# From One Addict to Another

## to Another

*One Man's Journey from the Depths of
Sexual Addiction to Freedom*

# Dann Aungst

ISBN: 978-0615806792

This is a true story. In some cases, names, locations, and other identifying information have been changed to protect the privacy of those involved.

To learn more, go to
www.addict2addict.org

# Table of Contents

**Pain**

# Introduction

*It was roughly eight years after my affair and in some ways things with my wife had gotten back to normal. Yet there was very little intimacy, and she still seemed to resent everything I did. There was still anger and pain over what had happened. Time had moved on but we never completely dealt with my actions. And now it was starting again. I had fallen back into looking at pornography and acting out. In the recent years and months, it had become more and more frequent. To this point I had been able to withstand going any further than this, but then one day I drove by a massage parlor and stopped. I went in, and let's just say that I experienced more than a massage. Afterward, I felt so disgusted with myself, which was unusual compared to the way I used to feel after acting out sexually. This time, I somehow recognized that my behavior wasn't actually about sex; rather, I knew that I was seeking to fill a void that could never be filled by this behavior. I felt so horrible that I drove immediately to a church looking for a priest to hear my confession. I was in a panic and knew I had to do this right now. I went to our usual church but no one was available, so I drove from church to church until I found a priest who could listen to my* confession. *After I'd finished, I told myself that it was over—I can't do this again.*

*Several months later, my wife learned that she had a sexually transmitted disease, evidence that I had strayed from our marriage yet again. She became completely unglued, and this time was talking divorce. My world was collapsing around me. I knew that Roxane was justified in every emotion she had and whatever action she took. What I couldn't believe was that I had done this again. I finally started to realize that, maybe, I have a problem.*

## Identifying the Problem

What was my problem? It was sexual addiction. It was clear now; I couldn't be in denial any longer. My behavior was preventing me from becoming the person I wanted to be, the person I needed to be, the Christian that my soul longed to be. It was destroying my family, my life, and I couldn't stop it.

Does any of this sound like you?

1. I've tried to stop masturbating or acting out sexually in other ways, but I just can't stop.

2. I try to justify my behavior, telling myself, "I need this right now" or "I deserve this."

3. I look at an attractive woman that is even slightly provocatively dressed and immediately begin fantasizing about her. Maybe it's not even sexual but just imagining what it would feel like to be in her company.

4. I fantasize about someone—maybe not even a real person, just someone I made up—to relax or escape from the stress of life.

5. I think that no one else struggles with these kinds of sexual thoughts.

6. I don't think anyone could possibly understand me.

7. I try to rationalize my thoughts by telling myself, "I'm a

guy. We all think this way; it's natural." But deep down, I know it's simply not true. Still I can't admit it to myself because then I couldn't ignore it anymore.

8. I'm so ashamed of myself and afraid that if anyone—even God—knew, really knew, what I have thought and done in the past that they would reject me. I fear that I am truly unlovable. I believe my secrets have to be kept secrets at any cost and must go with me to my grave.

If you answer yes to one or more of the above questions, it's important to know that you are not alone and that others could and do understand. I understand; I was there. Every question was a yes for me. Millions of other men have faced these same struggles with sexual thoughts and behavior. It's just not something we talk about. I used to think "If only others knew the truth … talk about real rejection."

In the pages ahead, I will share my own story and struggles with sexual addiction. I'll discuss how and why I think it started, what I think caused it, and why all of that doesn't really matter. I'll also recount my journey toward recovery—from the depths of sexual addiction to freedom and peace. In the book, I'll speak somewhat in generalities about my "acting out," but it's important to recognize that people who are sexual addicts act out in different ways; you may or may not relate to the behavior I describe. But the fact that we do act out, and the fact that we feel helpless and alone as a result, are the similarities that link all addicts together.

## Why I Wrote This Book

I wrote this book for many reasons. One reason was to offer other sexual addicts a real story that they can relate to. In my own efforts to learn more about sexual addiction and to understand, I have found a lot of material that is educational— material that provides psychological help, material that helps guide you through understanding the process of addiction, the history of addictions, etc. However, in all the books I have looked through, nothing compared with what happens when you're face-to-face with another addict and sharing your stories. Nothing compared to the learning and healing that can occur when talking with, or listening to, another addict. Miracles begin to happen when addicts realize that there is someone else who can relate to them, someone who truly understands what they're going through.

This power of sharing is illustrated in a story that someone in my support group told me at the beginning of my recovery:

*There was a group of several men who were Vietnam war POWs. When they returned from the war, they had a very difficult time adjusting to life at home and getting back to "normal." The soldiers were distant from their families; they withdrew emotionally from family and any regular activity. They couldn't hold jobs and many had severe depression. Significant amounts of counseling and help to get them to cope all failed. It wasn't until several of the POWs were put together in a group and began to talk about their experiences that the healing began. In this group, they each shared their stories and began to see what it was like for others who walked in their shoes, and they saw that someone else really understood what they went through and what they felt. When this happened, remarkable healing took place.*

I want to make it clear from the start that I am simply an addict. I am not a counselor or a psychologist; I do not have any training in the mental health profession.

This book is not a textbook.

This book is not an educational tool.

This book is not a psychological outline of addiction.

This book has nothing to do with any kind of Twelve Step process.

Instead, this book is a candid discussion with you, the reader—whom I assume is an addict, or is at least questioning whether you might be one—from me, the writer, speaking the way one addict would talk to another. Speaking from someone who truly understands what you are going through; someone who has been there; someone who understands your pain; someone who accepts you as you are, precisely where you are at, both spiritually and emotionally.

Again, I am not educated in the field of sexual addiction other than from my own experience. I am someone who has struggled with sexual addiction for most of my life, or at least for forty years. In recent months, I have found healing, I have found purpose, and I have found relief and through this I have learned a tremendous amount about myself. Through this healing and relief, I have seen that it is God who has guided me through this difficult time. I have received guidance as a result of my prayers over the despair I felt from being out of control with this addiction. I am telling my personal story because it has become clear to me that God wants me to tell others where I have been and to speak to you with a passion to let you know that you are not alone. You are understood, and there can be relief from where you are, as well as the feeling of true love beyond what you ever imagined.

I'm told sexual addiction is the darkest and most uncontrollable of addictions. Often, the symptoms are not visible to outsiders and the addiction gets progressively worse with time. The more time you spend in active addiction, the more you need to "fill the hole" within, a hole that you may not even realize is there; it gets bigger and bigger and your attempts to control it become less and less effective. The ways in which we act out become increasingly risky and dangerous. With sexual addiction, your downhill spiral can start with a single thought or even an event that makes you feel rejected or unworthy. It's the easiest addiction to escape with—you can disappear mentally, emotionally, and psychologically and no one even knows. I remember reading somewhere that an expert compared sexual addiction to a form of schizophrenia. Both sex addicts and schizophrenics have multiple realities and sometimes it is difficult to distinguish between them. These realities can easily "blend" together. As I said, I have battled with this addiction for over forty years. In this battle, the only relief and healing that I have experienced came with the peace and grace of our Lord Jesus Christ. In my journey toward recovery, I've discovered what it means to have true faith. God has put on my heart—and quite literally, I believe that God has asked me to share with other addicts—that there is hope, that there is someone who understands them on an emotional and spiritual level without judgment but with compassion and understanding. The beliefs that they are unlovable, that no one could understand them, and that others and even God would reject them if their indiscretions became known, THESE ARE ALL LIES! And these lies are even bigger than the ones that you tell others in order to hide what you do. My desire in this book is to tell you that you are not alone. And most of all, as much as you may doubt it, to tell you that God is with you, right now, at your side and He loves you perfectly and unconditionally—no questions asked.

If you don't believe in God or doubt He really cares, especially about you, know that I understand. All I ask is that you read my story and let me pray for you.

As this book is titled *From One Addict to Another*, I will occasionally throughout the book speak directly to you, a fellow addict. These sections are called "Addict to Addict." In these sections, I will offer tips or suggestions based on my own or the experience of others in recovery from sexual addiction. For the most part, however, I will simply share my story, as I've found the greatest discovery about myself and my greatest healing came from the direct sharing from, and to, other addicts. I hope that nonaddicts who read this will gain a better understanding of the disease and the addiction. That said, I believe that unless you struggle with sexual addiction yourself, you will never fully understand what an addict goes through.

I hope that my story and experiences will lead others who know deep down that they have a problem to seek help. I pray that it will help those who have not been able to bring themselves to tell anyone about their struggles or who have been too embarrassed to seek out a support group or counseling to finally find the courage to step out and begin the healing process of recovery. You already know you can't beat it alone. Now it's time to recognize that you do not have to be bound and chained by this addiction. There is hope.

# My Early Story

# Chapter 1

## Memories from My Childhood and Youth

I was born in Michigan and grew up in a small town called Otisville. I was born on April Fools' Day, which I guess was an appropriate launch for what was to come.

I have very limited memories of events from my early years and have even more memory gaps when it comes to my parents, especially my mother. I do remember a few friends in the neighborhood whom I played with regularly. And I have a few memories of school, but very little of my home life. It seems that most of the things I do remember are events that were negative or painful. For example, I remember being in trouble once and my mom chasing me around the house with a flyswatter to spank me. I also remember being at a carnival and breaking my front tooth on a candy apple as well as the classic falling off of my bike and getting really skinned up. I don't recall what my day-to-day life was like as a child, especially my interactions with my family—which included my mother, my father, and my brother—with only a few exceptions.

My parents were smokers back then and I have a faint memory of being in my crib and my mother accidently dropping cigarette ashes on me. I don't see how I could remember something from so early on; maybe I was told that it happened at a later time. Either way, it might be a small piece of the puzzle as to why I felt rejected and worthless from early on in life.

For most of my childhood, I was very skinny and bony. My mother once told me that when I was a toddler, she used to flinch when I would climb on her lap because the bones in my knees and elbows would poke her. While I don't remember the flinching, I do remember feeling uneasy around my mom, unworthy, even unwanted and rejected. Knowing now how unpleasant it was for her to hold me, I simply conclude that she didn't provide much physical attention to me.

To this day, I have this picture of myself wandering around alone in an empty house with no one to care for me. I know that was not the actual case, but for whatever reason, it's the memory I have.

I never felt "connected" with my mother or with anyone else in my family. My dad worked a lot, often on the afternoon and night shifts, so he wasn't around much during my early years. The memories I have with him are mostly from when I was a teenager or older. Our interactions were not negative; he just didn't have a lot of influence on me. While I'm sure I didn't understand it then, there was no feeling of acceptance or being wanted. I felt I was not lovable.

It seemed that whenever I got hurt or complained about a pain, my mom would just call me names. I really felt small when she did that. She would dismiss my feelings, or I felt I didn't have permission to feel bad about anything, leaving me to fend for myself and having to stuff my feelings. I felt from a very early age that my mother loved me only because she was supposed to—it was her duty as my mother—but not because she chose to, or because I deserved it.

I just never seemed to measure up. One example I can remember was when I was around eight years old. I was in Cub Scouts and even though I was just getting over some type of eye infection, I was supposed to go with the Scouts somewhere for the day, a city cleaning project or something like that. I was at the local community center a few blocks from home ready to go for the day, but I still didn't feel good. I remembered that my mom said if my eye started to bother me again, I should tell the scoutmaster and then just come home. So I told him how I felt and that my mom had said it was okay to leave, and I walked home. When I got there, I told my mom what had happened. But rather than asking how I was or comforting me or anything like that, all she did was call me a pantywaist because I didn't stick it out. Talk about rejection and feeling worthless!

Even though I was not adopted, I compare the way I felt to what they call the "China baby syndrome." Here's a description I ran across one day on the Internet:

*Children adopted from China have experienced the loss of their birthmothers and physical abandonment. Most have suffered deprivation of physical attention in varying degrees. These conditions interfere with the capacity to form secure attachments. Secure attachment forms when a child's physical and emotional needs are consistently met during the first 2 years of life. Because the child trusts that their parent will be there, they will internalize an image of their world as safe, stable, and dependable. They will develop independence while at the same time maintaining a connection with their parents. The child will learn to engage in mutually enjoyable interactions where the interaction itself is the end goal.*

*Reactive Attachment Disorder (RAD) is any disruption in attachment resulting in a child's failure to form a SECURE bond/attachment with a parental figure. The most securely attached people are confident, high-functioning individuals with a strong sense of self-worth, highly developed empathy and the ability to engage in healthy, mutually enhancing relationships, both within and beyond their immediate families. Unattached people commonly show characteristics of people without empathy or conscience, unable to relate to others except as objects to meet their needs. . . .*

*What it means is that the child's brain has been programmed to protect them from pain, thus preventing the child from giving and receiving love. The child will need specific treatment to learn how to do this.*

That pretty much explains how I feel in a nutshell. I have a very difficult time connecting with people; I tend to be a loner or antisocial. I feel I don't belong or am out of place when in groups. I remember even feeling like God made a mistake when I was born; I had no reason to be here.

# Chapter 2

## Creating the
## Perfect Friend—Kelly

When I was about six or seven, I created an imaginary friend. Her name was Kelly. She had long brown hair and I thought she was very cute. Why a girl rather than a boy for an imaginary friend I have to assume was the need for a loving female figure in my life.

I was one of those kids in school who was always chosen last for the dodge ball team, was picked on and made fun of, and was the weakest kid in gym class. In general, I was an outcast, or at least that's what I believed.

Kelly was the perfect friend to me. When playing alone, I would imagine Kelly picking me first to be on her team and we would always win. She made me feel like I was worth something; she was with me because she *wanted* to be. Although she was imaginary, Kelly helped to fill that void of not belonging or being unwanted. However, this wasn't a conscious decision at the time. I have distinct memories of being on the playground in elementary school and imagining Kelly was with me. I never told anyone about her or dared to talk out loud with her. Her existence was something I kept to myself.

I don't believe I created Kelly to resemble any of my classmates or anybody else I knew. She came purely from my imagination and I clung to her; thinking of her somehow made me feel more accepted. At the beginning I'm not sure I even realized that she wasn't real. I just remember her being there.

Throughout elementary school, Kelly stayed in the back of my mind, and I thought of her as my best friend. Actually, for years Kelly played a key part in helping me maintain my sanity. She was with me all the time. I would imagine her being there when I got out of bed in the morning and would think of her when going to sleep at night. I would frequently daydream about her or seek comfort from her when life was tough or unpleasant. Before puberty, my fantasies involving Kelly were not sexual; she was just someone who cared, someone who admired me for who I was, someone who loved me unconditionally.

# Chapter 3

## Awakening Sexuality—
## My First Exposure to Pornography

I must have been around ten or eleven years old when I was first exposed to porn. I was with a couple of friends when we went to the house of another boy who was a few years older than we were. The older boy pulled out a magazine from a group of other magazines that his dad had hidden. We looked through it with amazement—we had never seen naked women before. We all talked about the images we saw in the way we imagined our fathers talked about such women, mostly with derogatory comments and disrespect. That's what we thought we were supposed to do as "young men."

A few years later, my friends and I began exploring other forms of pornography. My best friend, Jim, had a sort of clubhouse over his garage. The garage was this huge barn with a high roof and an upstairs. They threw some carpet in it, added some old furniture and lights, and it became the perfect place for us to hang out. We had a rock band and so we would bring our instruments up there to practice and then spend the night like a campout. A bunch of us would stay there for the weekend or an entire week in the summer.

One night, I arrived at the clubhouse and Jim and another friend were already there. They had a reel-to-reel projector and were showing a silent movie that was X-rated. It was the first movie like this that we had ever seen. We must have watched it ten times that night, over and over. When we finally went to bed, I couldn't get the images out of my mind; I seemed to be fixated on them. Seeing the closeness of the man and woman created a deep craving in me—not necessarily for sex, but for the feeling of being wanted and desired. When I went home the next day, I was still thinking about that movie and those images. Even today, probably thirty-five years later, I can still remember the images from that movie. In my mind, watching that X-rated movie was the beginning of my addiction; it was where I first became fixated on images and thoughts of women. The physical acts portrayed in the movie at the time represented for me what it was like to be desired and loved. These were feelings that I was sadly lacking but didn't know it. I had Kelly, but she wasn't real; this was a real movie, with real people. Though it was distorted in a perverted sexual way, it still represented something I craved, a form of love and acceptance. I guess my innate humanness knew that a physical act of sex (or lovemaking) was the ultimate form of feeling accepted, desired, and respected. While this is true, what I saw was not what God had designed for us, but I didn't know that. All I knew was that I wanted it; I needed it.

The movie was a turning point for me. After seeing it, I became obsessed with sexually explicit magazines and photos. This was before the Internet and we were too young to get into adult movie houses, so our porn consumption was limited to magazines or photos from magazines. I never looked to see if my dad had any magazines like this hidden in our house, but I would steal them or tear out pages from the ones my friends had. I used to go to my friend Jim's house for days at a time in the summer, and occasionally I'd make an excuse to go up to his clubhouse alone, where I would quickly tear out some new pictures to take home. I would typically fantasize or look at these magazines and masturbate, sometimes once every few days, sometimes twice a day. I never really thought about why I was doing it. I do seem to remember there being a sense of shame that went along with it from the beginning, but I believe I just recorded it as embarrassment and hoped I wouldn't get caught.

During this time, Kelly grew stronger in my imagination. I "needed" her more and more. Only now, the relationship turned sexual—not always, but frequently. She gave me the attention that I needed, or that I thought I needed. Throughout most of my teenage years she was, in effect, my girlfriend. I didn't have the confidence to ask a real girl out, at least not until my senior year of high school.

# Chapter 4

## High School and My First Girlfriend

A girl named Kim was my first real girlfriend. She was the first girl I ever kissed, and emotionally I fell pretty fast. Here was this person, a real-life girl who actually liked me. I became obsessed with her. I saw her every day at school, called her every day, saw her every weekend, and so on. I couldn't get enough. Our sexual relationship never grew beyond kissing, as I think we were both too scared to do anything more, but I sure wanted to. It wasn't a hormone thing; rather, by then I felt that something sexual would bring the ultimate closeness, the ultimate level of acceptance.

Ultimately, I suffocated this girl with my neediness and after about six months, she broke up with me. I was devastated. I needed this type of attention so bad, and now it was not only yanked away from me but done so with rejection—the exact opposite of what I needed and what I thought I was getting closer to. Instead of completely falling apart, I turned again to Kelly, but it wasn't the same anymore. There wasn't any real physical touch. Even though our relationship was not sexual, Kim had provided attention that was real rather than created by my thoughts. But Kelly was all I had now. She quickly became my status quo.

Throughout most of high school, I felt like an outcast—the "ugly nerd." I wasn't athletic but I was smart. School was easy for me, but that wasn't what gave a person value, at least not then. The girls didn't care for the smart ones, just the jocks, and I was the furthest thing from it. I didn't fit in with anyone.

I had just two friends during high school, Mark and Jim. Jim was the one with the clubhouse above the garage. Both Mark and Jim played guitar, and I played drums. We formed our own little three-person music group, which was our escape. It was one place where I felt some sort of belonging.

My infatuation with porn magazines and related behaviors increased during high school. I wanted another girlfriend so bad. I would have taken anyone, even someone who would just act as if they liked me. I only got the nerve to ask out one other girl during high school and she turned me down—talk about a kick in the teeth. I figured the only way to avoid that pain again was to not ask! High school ended up pretty lonely, so I just stuck to my two friends, music, and Kelly.

# Chapter 5

## College and Discovering Sex

College was interesting to say the least. I went to a private university about an hour and a half from home. The university had apartment buildings instead of dorms for resident students. As I freshman, I was assigned to an apartment with two seniors. One of them, Ben, was a real partier. The other roommate didn't really care much about partying and wasn't around a lot.

Ben was a good looking guy, with the right attitude for being a "player." He was always setting up parties on the weekends. It seemed his goal in life was to get laid. We had bunk beds in our room, and it seemed like every Friday and Saturday night he had a girl in his bed. Now when I look back at that time and the little I knew about Ben and his broken family, I have to wonder if he was a sexual addict too. He definitely had senioritis; I don't ever remember him doing homework.

A few weeks into the school year, Ben found out I was a virgin. He then made it his mission to get me laid before the school year was out. Before long, mission accomplished. I remember that once this "line," so to speak, had been crossed, the whole game changed for me. The very short time I spent with the girl my roommate set me up with awoke a feeling inside me of being desired and accepted. A real person wanted me like my imaginary friend Kelly did. Even though with this girl it was just sex and no real relationship developed, it didn't matter. For a brief period, I had felt satiated and yet I couldn't get enough—I had to have that feeling again. Sex became all I could think about. While I didn't have any more "success" the next couple of years at college, it sure wasn't due to a lack of trying.

During this period, I watched a lot of X-rated movies because I could get them and I was alone so much. I would rent movies several times a week, sometimes several at a time, and act out. I really had no clue what this behavior meant; I didn't think about it at all. It was just something I would do to entertain myself since I had few friends. Looking back at all these movie rentals and activities that I was engaged in, however, I can see that it was definitely compulsive. However, I wouldn't say it was uncontrollable because I never tried to control it.

After my third year at this college, I changed my major and transferred to another school. This was the first time I lived alone. Soon after the move, I met a woman named Beth and we became sexually active almost immediately. At last, I thought I had found someone who accepted me—her willingness to have sex proved it, and it was proven frequently. Toward the end of the school year, Beth decided to move to California to be closer to her family and deal with some family issues. This was not acceptable for me. I had finally found someone and something to fill the void I felt inside; now I could not live without her. So I transferred schools again, uprooting myself and moving to California too. I followed Beth out about three weeks after she left. She was staying with relatives, and they graciously invited me to live with them until I found my own place. When I got there, however, things were different between us. Beth was acting kind of hostile. We never had sex again and eventually broke up. I was devastated but somehow moved on. Years later, thinking back on that time, I realize that Beth had most likely met someone else during the three-week period before I arrived in California. Perhaps she was starving for acceptance as much as I was.

For the next several years I was alone. I thought several times about fulfilling my sexual desires by hiring a prostitute, but I was too scared to and, besides, I didn't have the money to do it. If I would have had the extra cash, I may have taken that chance. With what I know now about sexual addiction, I'm sure that would have pushed me into the next phase of my addiction. Until now, my insatiable cravings were only for the physical attention that I had received so far, and when that wasn't there (or even sometimes when it was), there were other methods of acting out sexually.

Today, I can clearly see that if I had taken that next step and hired a prostitute, I would have gone over the edge. I can see myself being the guy who sells everything he has—maybe even stealing—just to get the money for the next hooker. I believe it was God's intervention that it never happened.

# The Slide Into
# Sex Addiction

# Chapter 6

## Roxane

A few years after I moved to California, I decided to work on my degree again and enrolled at a university in the San Fernando Valley. This was where I met Roxane, the woman who would eventually become my wife. When we first met, I remember thinking that she seemed like one of the nicest and sweetest people I had ever met. She was a little overweight but that didn't really matter, as she was very pretty and had a great smile and personality.

We had a computer class together, so I saw her several times each week. I wanted to go out with her but was too insecure to ask for a date. Instead, I asked her if she wanted to study together. I thought that was safe and had a low risk of rejection. Plus, it gave me a chance to spend some time with her and to feel out whether I could risk asking her out on a date.

We did get together to study and ended up talking a lot. She was very pleasant and comfortable to be around. When I finally got up the nerve to ask her out, she said yes and we started dating. Our relationships progressed and became very serious for both of us quite quickly. I was happy about that, because once I started feeling accepted by someone, I always wanted more. We spent a lot of time together between school and dates and just hanging out at her place.

With Roxane, I had met someone whose need for love and acceptance seemed similar to mine. While we weren't sexual at this point, her emotional needs likely met mine and this fueled a fast-paced relationship. While I was dating Roxane, Kelly all but disappeared as my companion and confidant. However, since our relationship wasn't yet sexual, porn and masturbation continued to be a regular part of my regimen.

After dating for only about six months, Roxane and I got engaged. We were together about a year and a half before we got married.

From the start, our marriage was okay but not fantastic. I know we both grew up struggling with a lot of rejection issues and, as a result, were very guarded over our hearts, making it difficult for us to open up and be very close to one another. Those rejection issues would be something that would ultimately create problems for us down the road. Our sex life was average, likely another casualty of our inability to open up and share ourselves as intimately as we should because of our personal issues.

My pattern of masturbation that began when I was a teen continued even after I got married, though it was less frequent. It became something that "I" wanted. It wasn't about Roxane; it was for me and my personal enjoyment. I think I knew it was probably wrong but rationalized it in my mind since I wasn't hurting anyone, or so I thought. Only years later did I realize that this behavior not only caused feelings of rejection for Roxane on the rare occasion she found out, but it was another selfish behavior that focused on me. It created (or continued) a self-culture of "it's all about me." By carrying out this behavior, I was much less likely to give of myself to someone—namely, my spouse—and more likely to take and always expect my way. And ultimately that led to more and more radical, risky, and selfish behavior that did create more distance in our marriage. When I had that inward self-vision, I was not looking at or attending to my spouse's needs, physically or emotionally. We did not connect and, as a result, our marriage suffered significantly. The very thing I needed—to be wanted, to be loved—I was in a strange way making impossible, because Roxane could not respond in love and attentiveness to me if I did not offer that to her. I was greatly contributing to the downward spiral of our marriage and creating a situation where my true needs would go unmet. The early stages of my acting out in our marriage, by masturbating, were actually counterproductive.

## Addict to Addict

Why do we think that when we get married all our problems will go away? We think this new woman whom we want to spend the rest of our lives with will solve everything, and we will no longer even desire to look at porn, act out, or see other women. We think our "inner hole" will be filled! Why doesn't it work like this when you get married? The answer is simple: the only thing that fills this hole is unconditional love, perfect love, merciful love, compassionate love, and it doesn't take long to find out that the person you married doesn't give you that. They can't! It's impossible. No human being can. *Only* the love of God, the Holy Spirit, and Jesus Christ can do this! You are looking in the wrong place to fill your true needs. Don't get me wrong, marriage is a wonderful thing, especially in God's overall plan, but it is not intended to fill the void deep within that we addicts compulsively seek to fill. Marriage is a union between two souls under God, but you still need God in the center! You have to surrender yourselves to God and surrender your marriage to God or you will never be completely filled and you will never know true peace.

Oh, I get it. This all sounds very simplistic. In a way it is, but it is a lifelong journey to actually do it. I think of it as what Christ said in the Bible when talking about childlike faith. I find that the more I can position myself in the mind of a child when looking at Christ, the easier it is to "get it." The world makes it too complicated; it gets in the way of truly surrendering or emptying yourself to God. But trust me, this is where we find true peace and true fulfillment. If you can get inside the simplistic mind of a child, empty yourself, and ask Jesus to come—and you are truly empty and surrendered without condition—He will fill you with love and intimacy to the point of tears.

---

At this point, God was really not a big part of my life. Roxane was Catholic, and so we got married in the Catholic Church and I attended Sunday services with her, but I was not Catholic myself. I grew up Methodist, though I don't remember actually going to church.

A few years after we got married, Roxane encouraged me to join a program for people who are interested in converting to Catholicism. The program, RCIA (Rite for Christian Initiation of Adults), helps non-Catholics learn about the Catholic Church and ultimately on Easter be confirmed as a Catholic. I went through the program with Roxane as my sponsor, and that next

Easter I was confirmed into the Catholic Church. Looking back, I realize that I only went through the motions of joining the church and it really didn't sink in what it was all about. I still didn't feel God in my life, nor did I feel worthy of Him.

# Chapter 7

## The Next Level of Addiction

A few years into our marriage, I started my own software company. The business became fairly successful, which was at least partially attributable to the time and effort I put into it. During this time, I came to believe that my work represented who I was and my value as a person; therefore, the more I worked, the more successful the business would become and the more value I would have as a person—or so I thought. It didn't actually work that way. But I was so caught up in and obsessed with the business that my work became another form of addiction. As with sex, the more I looked for it, the more I thought I needed it and the more I attempted to get. But it never seemed to fill the void. Of course, at that time, I didn't see this or understand why I was behaving as I was. I didn't know that I was working so much because I was trying to find what was missing in my life or because it was going to make me feel like I was good enough. I only knew that I had a drive to fill something or chase something—I didn't realize what I was chasing. Strangely though, one addiction didn't replace the other. Rather, they both compounded. But neither method of "chasing" produced the desired results—neither my sex nor my work addiction filled the void that I was yet to discover even existed.

As time went on and my company grew, I began meeting other individuals in the software industry. One person I met from another company, Luke, was not a competitor but was in a similar area of software, and we quickly began combining marketing efforts on our products. We began attending trade shows together around the country—Las Vegas, New York, and so on—and sharing an exhibit booth at these events to cut costs and to benefit our customers, since we offered complementary products.

Before long, I learned that Luke was a playboy of sorts. One time when we were working at an event in Las Vegas, he invited me to go for a ride with him so he could introduce me to something that he thought I would enjoy. We ended up at a brothel about ninety minutes outside of Vegas. I remember being very nervous at the time, thinking, "I can't believe I'm about to do this." But Luke encouraged me to go ahead, saying, "Who is going to ever know?" So I did. This was the first time I cheated on my wife with another person, and the experience set me off down a dangerous slope of things yet to come. On future business trips with Luke, we would sometimes patronize other places like this (he always seemed to know where they were). Now I truly had a double life. In the introduction, I mentioned that the behavior in sex addiction can look like schizophrenia. This was now coming to play in my life: married life versus pornography, masturbation, an imaginary person, fantasies, and now brothels! This was f***d up.

I think that for the longest time, I believed all the lies I was telling myself and others. They were rationalization for what I wanted to do, what "I" needed. But I needed to keep my life separate in order to support them. They weren't lies in that other world, but I never said that then.

Although I had converted from a non-practicing Methodist Christian to a practicing Catholic, I still had two different mental lives. But now that I was attending church more, I began to be more aware of the sin I was committing. I always knew it, but before it had been much easier to rationalize. It's amazing what the stronghold of an addiction can do. In the back of my mind, I knew I was living a lie, going to church in a state of severe mortal sin, but I was able to bury it and ignore it in the name of selfishness. It wasn't until much later that my two realities would come crashing together.

It was about five years into our marriage at this point, and I was not getting the love and intimacy that I needed, that I craved. Even though we were having sex, it wasn't working for me—it wasn't enough for me. It wasn't Roxane's fault; I was the one who didn't understand what I truly needed. I was truly oblivious to what was missing in my life and why I was doing what I was doing. I didn't recognize the emptiness I felt inside, the emptiness I was desperately trying to fill. Roxane was there, my wife and partner in life . . . but our relationship just didn't fill the unrecognizable void deep within. It was a blind craving that drove me silently. These ugly attempts to fill it—my acting out—served as five-second breaks from the emptiness but then left me with a stronger craving, a bigger hole to fill. I had mentally separated this behavior from who I otherwise was so well that it truly didn't seem like me. It was another person who was acting out. This thinking helped assuage my guilt, making it manageable. And my delusional thinking convinced me that since it "really wasn't me," my two worlds would never collide and Roxane would never know.

Today, looking back at this time in my life, I can see that all my rationalizing—"It's not really me," "You deserve this," and "She'll never know"—were all lies! I realize now that I must have had an underlying sense that my actions were wrong and could hurt her; otherwise, I wouldn't have known to hide them. But I couldn't see it then. At the time, I just felt that there was a hole inside of me that I had to fill at any cost. The need was like needing air; I thought I would suffocate and die without it. Fortunately, God knew a way that I could finally fill that hole, and He would allow me to eventually crash so I could turn to Him, broken and empty, where He could make the difference.

# Chapter 8

## The Affair

A few years later, a woman named Tiffany began working for my company. After a few months she began to make comments about how she admired what I did, the way I ran the company, and she offered compliments about me personally. You could say she gave all the right strokes to my ego and I relished the feeling. Looking back, I can see that I was so hungry for acceptance and anything close to what seemed like unconditional love that I was willing to do anything to get it or accept it from anyone.

One day when we were alone in a company warehouse, what had been admiration and flirtation became something more. By this time in my life, I had been with prostitutes, wrapped up in my own fantasies, and obsessed with pornography; in general, I had become blind and numb to the idea that I could be taking advantage of another person who seemed interested and who admired me. I was so overwhelmed with the attention I was receiving and my need for it that I not only accepted her advances, I encouraged them. Soon I was having a full-fledged affair with Tiffany. Within a couple of weeks of starting the affair,

I felt so good about myself, like I hadn't felt in quite a while. This was a woman who gave me all the right strokes; she looked up to me and seemed to be genuinely interested who I was, which built up my self-esteem. I had cast my morals aside and so was willing to take advantage of whatever she was offering me. I rationalized my actions, convincing myself that I deserved this; I deserved this type of attention. We became infatuated with one another, and I blindly fell deeper and deeper into the affair. I couldn't see what I was actually doing. My actions were completely selfish. Once again, in my mind I saw this as a separate life—I separated what I was doing from my life with Roxane and from my marriage. When I was living one life, it was almost as if the other didn't exist.

Tiffany was also married with a family. But after we had been together for a few weeks, we both thought we had found what we really wanted from a partner and began to talk about leaving our families for each other. We developed plans for breaking the news to our spouses. Because my marriage had not been so great anyway, I thought that the moment I told Roxane that I wanted out, she would say, "Wow, I'm glad you're the first one to say it" and it would be that simple. I wasn't planning on telling her about Tiffany; I was just hoping we could agree to go our separate ways and then I would introduce Tiffany into the rest of my life at a later time. So I contacted two of Roxane's and my closest friends and asked them to come over to our house to be Roxane's support when I told her I wanted out of the marriage. These were friends whom I had told at earlier times that I was unhappy in my marriage. When these two individuals met with Roxane and me, we sat and talked about what I was feeling and what I wanted. To my surprise, Roxane did not feel the same way. All of a sudden, I had to think fast and explain why the marriage wasn't working for me and convince Roxane that I had valid reasons for wanting out. We all talked for a while and it was apparent that Roxane was very upset but was trying not to show it. After our friends left, Roxane turned and ran upstairs into our bedroom, and I heard her let out a wailful cry like I had never heard before. Only then did it begin to sink in what I was actually doing, and I realized that I had really hurt her. I was now in a panic and didn't know what to do. Even knowing that I was crushing my wife, though, I was too selfish to stop my plan. Instead, I just worked harder to justify going forward with what "I" wanted. Looking back, I can see that the emptiness in my soul fed my selfish actions. I was coming from the same place and had the mind-set of an addict. Any single event in and of itself may not look like an addiction, but when viewing the bigger picture and considering my history, my actions here were signs that the addiction was progressing. But at the time, I was in a self-preserving mode—I had tunnel vision and only saw the current event in front of me, which was bad enough.

## Addict to Addict

Be on guard and avoid setting yourself up for a "slip." For alcoholics, this means staying out of bars and other drinking environments; for sex addicts, this means being cautious around women you are not in a relationship with. Don't flirt or even have conversations of a personal level with female friends or acquaintances. And, when possible, avoid spending time alone with other women, even co-workers, friends, or acquaintances. Also consider whether it's wise to have female friends. For a married man, this time alone with any woman opens the "opportunity" for emotional connection. Then it's downhill from there. Even an emotional connection with another woman without physical relations is inappropriate and dangerous. If your heart is attached to someone else, you have no chance of creating the intimacy required in a marriage. It is impossible for you to be "present" with your wife if you are focused on someone else. Bluntly, if you think otherwise, you are lying to yourself.

I knew a married man who long ago had an affair. Several years later, I ran into him at a restaurant where he was having dinner with a woman he said was a client. There they were: alone, eating, and sharing a bottle of wine. I said hello, and he introduced me to this woman. This hit me right between the eyes. It was an extremely dangerous situation, an invitation for things to start down the wrong path. If you think you can handle such a situation yourself, think again.

---

I continued to insist that I wanted to leave the marriage and move out. Roxane's reaction again surprised me: she started working harder than ever to try to make me happy and convince me to stay. Now I was really confused and didn't know what to do. For a time, I went along with it, and at home acted as if we were trying to work it out while still carrying on the affair. My selfish heart still really wanted to leave. As time went on, it became harder and harder to stay at home. I simply couldn't face how hard Roxane was trying to change and make things better when I just wanted out. She was interfering with my plans. I decided that the only thing I could do now was to rent an apartment and actually move out. Then, I figured, I would no longer be influenced by her niceness and efforts to change. It still didn't work. It was then that I realized if I really wanted her to release me, I would have to tell her about the affair. She had always told me that she could never forgive me for being unfaithful. So a few days later I told her what was actually going on. At first it seemed like she was again crushed, and I could hardly stand to see what I was doing to her. I just wanted to get it all over with. Yet, as I started to leave, she began pleading with me to stay, saying that she could look past my affair and that we could work it out. She began weeping and begging me not to go. This was not working out at all, I thought. When I told her about my affair, I expected her to be so mad that she would kick me out and it would finally be over. But for some reason she still wanted me. Being the selfish asshole I was at the time, I chose to leave anyway. After all, I knew what I wanted. (Side personal note: When I was writing this, I was astounded to fully realize the devastation and destruction I had been causing Roxane but was oblivious to; I was destroying her. I was so messed up.)

Since I had told Roxane that I wanted to leave her, multiple friends who were very close to our family came over to try to talk me out of it. Most of them didn't know about the affair or what was really going on. And I didn't tell them about it. I would just offer all kinds of excuses about why things weren't working and why I wanted out of the marriage. I was resolved that no one was going to change my mind.

Several of my close male friends invited me to join them at a Christian men's retreat that was coming up. I, of course, refused their offers. Inside I knew I didn't want to go there and face what I was really doing. On some level, I was also afraid that somebody might affect me and change my mind about leaving Roxane. My friends told me that if I changed my mind about going, there would be a place for me at the retreat. I continued to think, "No way am I going to that."

After I had finally moved out of our home and into my own apartment, it was Tiffany's turn to tell her family that she was leaving. Although her husband, too, was crushed upon hearing the news, she still wanted to go forward with our plan and end her marriage.

At my company, a close friend of our family, Mary, worked for me. Up until this point, I had kept pretty quiet at work about my relationship with Tiffany and what was going on with Roxane, but Mary was one person I had confided in. Of course, Mary had only heard my distorted side of the story, but she seemed to be supporting my decision.

It was now the Thursday before the men's retreat (that I wasn't going to). Tiffany and I were working in different areas of the building when an employee named Marcy came into my office. Now Marcy was one of those individuals who was very spiritual; she used to tell people that she could talk to God and she would get visions and messages from God. We all thought she was kind of a nutcase and never took seriously what she said. When she came into my office that day, she had evidently heard about my affair with Tiffany and our plans, because she told me about a vision she had had the night before that was about us. She said that God showed her what would happen to our children if we followed through with our plan, the pain that we would cause others, and the damage that would ensue—not just emotional damage but things like our families getting hurt or killed. To all of this, I responded, "Okay, Marcy. Thank you for letting me know" and said she could go back to work. Although I still thought this woman was a wacko, I brought Tiffany into my office and told her about Marcy's vision. She seemed a little bit concerned about it and suggested that we spend some time discussing it at lunch. Now before we went to lunch, one of my friends who had invited me to the retreat called and said that I was still welcome to come to the retreat this weekend and that we could drive together. He made a point to tell me that there would be no judgment and he was there to listen if I wanted to talk. I told him thanks anyway, but I didn't plan on going so he should just go ahead without me tomorrow and that was it.

At lunchtime, Tiffany and I went to my apartment to talk over what Marcy had said about her vision. This is where things really started to get interesting. Tiffany was visibly shaken by it, obviously scared by what Marcy had said. She told me that she felt like something was going wrong. I reminded her that this was what we both wanted, and we just needed to follow through with our plan. Tiffany wasn't sure and so, as strange and warped as it seems, we decided to pray about it—we wanted to pray that we could continue in our life of sin. We were so selfish and blind that we thought we could ask God to help us go ahead and do what we wanted to do while alleviating the pain we were causing those around us and keeping our children safe. What a joke! To actually pray for help in carrying out our sin and protecting the people whom we were hurting? This was utter disillusionment. But pray we did. We asked God to protect our families and our kids from enduring too much hurt from our actions. I began to get emotional, as we were deciding something that I wanted very badly. I actually told God that I would do anything He asked of me if He would just help us to do this and keep our kids safe. I technically gave God my consent to do whatever He wanted to in my life. Oddly enough, it was the first time that I had ever completely surrendered my life to God and gave Him permission to do anything He chose, but I did it so I could get my way. Little did I know He would do exactly as I asked, but not in the way I expected. As soon as we said our prayer, a faint image of a stop sign appeared in my mind. I dismissed it, not thinking that it meant anything, and just continued on. At around 1 p.m., Tiffany and I returned to work separately. When I got back to the office, my friend Mary came in almost immediately; she was visibly disturbed, upset and almost crying. She told me that something had come over her and, although she felt very strange about doing so, she had to tell me that what I was doing was wrong. She explained that she didn't know why she didn't feel this way before but that during lunch, something came over her and made her feel like she had to tell me this. I told her that it was okay, to not worry about it and go back to work. As she was leaving, Marcy came in my office again; I wondered what crackpot thing she was going to say now. She told me she felt that God was working and the black cloud that she had sensed over us was going to lift. I had no clue what she was talking about, but I said, "Okay, Marcy, whatever you think. Thank you," and she left. Immediately after she left, another employee, Denise, came in. Denise was a friend of Tiffany's and so she also knew about our relationship. Denise was extremely disturbed and crying. She said, "I don't know why I came in here and I hope you don't fire me, but I just had to tell you that you can't keep doing what you are doing. You have to stop. I don't know why I had no control and I hope you don't fire me." I assured Denise that it was okay, that she wouldn't be fired, and that she could go ahead and go back to work.

By then the image of a stop sign that I had dismissed earlier was growing more vivid in my mind; it was starting to distract me. A couple of minutes later, Tiffany came back in my office, very upset, and said, "It feels like everything is falling apart. I don't know what is going on. I don't know what to do." I told her everything was okay and not to worry about it, that it would all be fine.

I started feeling really weird at this point. Something was clearly happening but I wasn't sure what. Then suddenly I knew that I needed to stop this whole thing and go back home. It was the weirdest experience I've ever had; it was almost like a scene from the *Twilight Zone*—one person after another coming in my office and telling me that I had to stop what I was doing. The affair had been going on for a while—why would they all do this now? Then it dawned on me: only a couple of hours earlier, I had prayed to God and asked Him to do whatever it took to keep people from getting hurt. Did He make all this happen? I wasn't really sure I believed in supernatural events like this; it seemed just too strange. But I couldn't deny the image of the stop sign in my head. I started accepting that this was a message and that I really did have to stop what I was doing and start doing what was right.

It was around four o'clock by then. I called Roxane and asked her if I could come over tonight so we could talk. She said that would be fine. That night, I told her a little bit about what had happened and that I had decided that I wanted to come home; I asked her if she would let me. She said she would as long as I agreed to attend the retreat this weekend. I agreed. She also told me that I needed to call Tiffany at that very moment and break it all off and tell her that she couldn't work with me anymore. It was a hard call to make, but I knew it was what I had to do. It was the right thing to do.

# Chapter 9

## The Gathering of Men Retreat

The very next day I had to keep my promise to go to the men's retreat. I called my friend Paul and told him that I wanted to go. I didn't tell him why I had changed my mind or that I had moved back home, nor had Roxane told anyone that I had come back home.

At about three o'clock, I met up with my Paul and we took off for the retreat center in the mountains. During the drive, I told him what had happened, we prayed a little, and he said he was just happy to have me back and that I had finally agreed to go. We got into town and met with some of our other friends at a restaurant and had dinner. When we arrived at the retreat center to check in, I was surprised to see my name on the list and that I had been assigned a room with my friends—I hadn't filled out an application or paid the deposit. The retreat started at seven o'clock. I had never been to an event like this and wasn't sure what to expect, but everyone seemed energized. I later learned that there were about 300 men at this retreat and everyone came to learn more about themselves. I was told that the retreat format basically comprised of one man giving a talk on a subject and then the audience breaking into small groups and discussing what the speaker said. There was one talk on Friday night; it seemed okay but nothing special at this point.

After the small-group exercise, there was a social time for the men to mingle and become better acquainted. Most of the men seemed to already know one another from previous retreats. It was like a reunion for them. Only a few of us had never been there before and were just getting a feel for what this was about. As I was walking around, a priest, whose name was Father Ken Leone, walked up to me, looked at my name badge, and said "Dann Aungst!" with exclamation and surprise in his voice. "I've been looking all over for you." He continued, "Jesus asked me to give this to you," and he handed me an envelope. I opened it to find this letter:

*Dann, there is so much I would like to tell you if only there were enough time. You are entering a very difficult time but it is also a time when you're going to learn a lot about Roxane, about yourself, and about me and my love for you.*

*Please be patient with yourself. This is not going to go away overnight. The wounds are deep but not fatal. There's much healing that needs to take place for your wife, your friends, yourself, and for our relationship.*

*The important thing though is that our relationship has begun. Let's go through this together; give me all of your hurt, your resentment, and your pain. I can take it! And I promise I will continue to love you.*

*There are big plans for you. If only you knew everything*

*that is still ahead. It is so important to begin this healing process. I will be here to help you. Please lean on me; use me. I will give you the strength and courage when you have nothing left.*

*You will discover that true strength comes from humility and true power comes from grace.*

*I will be here to help you but the work is up to you.*

*Your Friend,*
*Jesus*

I about fell on the floor. I turned around and looked for the priest; I wanted to know who gave him this letter and where it came from. But he was nowhere to be seen. My head was spinning. I had decided to come to the retreat at the last minute—no one even knew that I had ended the affair and moved back home except Paul and he only found out on the ride up here. I started examining the letter to try to figure out where it could have come from. It was just too amazing to have actually come from Jesus— although considering the outrageous events that happened after my prayer and complete surrender just the day before, it almost seemed to make sense. I continued to look at the letter. What I found odd was that my name and Roxane's name were spelled correctly. I have an extra "N" in my name and Roxane's name is short an "N" from the traditional spellings. So whoever wrote this had to have known us. Yet nobody who knew us could have written this letter. Nobody knew I was coming. And nobody knew that I had ended the affair. I was simply blown away.

The weekend retreat continued. I found a lot of worthwhile information in many of the talks. I began thinking about myself in ways that I had never looked at before. Men spoke openly about their emotional wounds and pain of the past. I, for the first time in my life, began to see that I had some of these same wounds and that I was not alone. I even began to get a glimpse of the damage I was inflicting and the emotional pain  I was causing my family. One man said, "We must transform our pain; otherwise we will transmit it." I never forgot this insightful statement, though I didn't really understand it until a few years later. Everything at the retreat revolved around Christ. The mere act of sharing our personal stories actually began to foster healing in some way. I had never experienced nor imagined that something like this was possible. However, since I was so new to everything that was being said, it only scratched the surface for me. I didn't "get" most of it, but it nonetheless awakened me to start to see things differently. It was a foundation for what was to come in the years ahead.

# Chapter 10

## Coming Home

It was Sunday evening when I came home from the weekend retreat. I felt better than I had in a long time—free of my hidden life. I had gone to confession at the retreat and afterward felt a huge weight lifted from my shoulders. I was ready to move on with life, only I didn't realize that I had yet to face the consequences of my actions.

It all kind of blew up when I came home. I was there, at the retreat, and Roxane was home alone for three days and two nights to think about everything that had happened and everything that might have happened. Almost immediately upon returning home, I was face-to-face with Roxane who was very angry and bitter. She started in on a barrage of questions: who else had I been with, had there ever been any other affairs, should she be tested for AIDS, and what else had I done? I wasn't prepared for this, but did my best to answer her questions. I disclosed the brothels and prostitutes I had visited while on business trips with Luke, along with other infidelities over the years. I just dumped it all out. I couldn't deal with the anger; I just wanted it all to stop.

She, quite reasonably, was irate at my answers to her probing questions. The magnitude of my disclosure set Roxane off on an extreme roller coaster of emotions. She went from rage and anger along with hours of crying to days of calm, when it seemed as if everything was okay. Then it would start all over again. I, of course, was not any comfort. I would just cringe and retreat emotionally and wait for her angry moments to pass. I did not yet understand why I had strayed from our marriage and acted out sexually. This was before I received the education and self-awareness to understand that I had felt unloved and unworthy and was seeking to fill that hole in any way possible. And when Tiffany came along, it felt so good to be appreciated and admired that I grabbed on to that feeling and to her like it was a lifeline. But at this point, all I knew was that I did what I did, and now it was over and I had come home. My not being able to explain my actions made the homecoming very difficult. All I remember is that Roxane pressured me, asking how I could have done these things and why she should believe that I wouldn't do anything like this again. My only response was, "Well, I came home, didn't I?" In retrospect, this was obviously not the right thing to say; it only seemed to make the situation worse. The reality was, I couldn't face what I had done to her—I was in complete denial of the pain I had caused. Yet every time I witnessed the anguish and sorrow in her, it revealed a bit more of the truth of what I had done, the actions I had taken in response to the pain I felt within. How could I deal with this? All I was capable of doing was reacting in anger, trying to defend myself. In truth, it was no defense; there was no answer, no way to justify what I had done. Over the many years of my life, I had done such a good job of building a wall to cover my own pain that I wasn't able to get in touch with it and, thereby, feel hers. This made for a long and difficult recovery.

Everything I did from that point forward was scrutinized.

Roxane monitored my email and forbade me to have any future relations with Luke. She always wanted detailed information on where I was going and how long I would be gone. There was no trust in our relationship, and there shouldn't have been. After many, many months and even a few years in some instances, the "leash" began to loosen. I don't think that it was because Roxane began to trust me; I think she just got tired of babysitting.

As time went on, the tension at home also seemed to get a little better. Or, more accurately, I think that Roxane learned to bury the pain I had caused and to just live life. That was okay with me, as I didn't really understand myself or the pain she felt.

Then one night I guess God decided it was time for me to open my eyes and grasp what I had done. At about 3 a.m., I got up to go to the bathroom. I went in and sat down in the dark, as I usually didn't like to turn the lights on in the middle of the night because it tended to wake me up too much. As I sat there, I suddenly felt immobilized as pictures entered my mind. I don't really want to say that it was a vision, but I'm not sure how else to describe it. I was shown three images. The first one was of the time when our friends were over and I was telling Roxane that I wanted to leave and didn't want to be married to her anymore. I saw her run up the stairs and slam the bedroom door and let out the wail that I spoke of earlier. Except this time, the vision was accompanied by what felt like a kick in the stomach. I felt what she felt. I thought I was going to throw up. I had never experienced anything so intense and so emotionally painful in my life. I've never even imagined anything could feel this way. Immediately after this scene, another vision came. It was of the time I had told Roxane about the affair. Again I felt overwhelmingly pain, loss, rejection, and just a sense of the world crashing down around me. And then in the third image, I was somehow hovering above our bedroom watching Roxane tell our children that Daddy has left and won't be coming back because he doesn't love us anymore.

That one was the worst of all. I felt the rejection and the pain that my children must have felt. I felt like I wanted to die. Roxane later told me that this last image never actually happened, but I think I was shown this to reveal the pain I had nonetheless inflicted on my children.

As quickly as they came, the images went away, and I got up and returned to bed. I ended up waking Roxane, because I was sobbing so hard I couldn't even talk. She asked me what was wrong and I eventually got out what I had just seen. We sat in bed together and cried for what seemed like hours. The images and the accompanying pain were so real to me that I knew I had felt what she experienced. I didn't know why this was happening, only that there was obviously something God wanted me to know.

# Chapter 11

## Biblical Counseling

Over the years, Roxane and I had seen several couples marriage counselors—some good, some not so good. Looking back, there was one who was really bad, but we didn't realize it at the time. She actually suggested we could help our marriage and spice things up by watching pornographic videos together. How incredibly inappropriate! I can hardly believe that a professional therapist could actually suggest such a thing. This is wrong in so many ways I can't even talk about it here—that's a book in and of itself! This counselor was one we worked with before and during the affair. Needless to say, she didn't help much.

About a year after the affair, though, we didn't hesitate when some of our friends, actually the ones who were present when I told Roxane I wanted to leave, told us about a very powerful marriage counseling experience they had done and recommended it to us. Called biblical counseling, the intensive one-week program consisted of meeting with a counselor for about four hours per day. We were also encouraged to stay in a hotel during this time so we could continue the experience after each day's sessions. At this point in our marriage, we both knew we needed something like this type of counseling. The problems we needed to address went way beyond my affair and other indiscretions.

Our counselor, John, was a very gifted person. He had a unique way of incorporating prayer and helping us feel connected with Jesus in the midst of the counseling sessions. Roxane and I were benefiting not only from John's counsel, but also from a prayer partner who sat in the back of the room and prayed for us throughout the entire counseling session. In no time at all, we forgot that the prayer partner was even there.

John spoke with a tone that was almost meditative. Right from the start of the first session, he seemed to speak directly to the child within each of us. The counseling format was different from what most people would think of as counseling; it was almost like a prayer or a conversation that he would lead us through. In a way, it was almost as if we were talking to Jesus, asking Him to reveal to us different pains and to help us forgive others who had hurt us. John started with Roxane. He suggested that she talk to the little girl inside herself and ask her what she's feeling—for example, does she feel alone or is she scared? I burst into tears. Those questions struck me to the core.

John then turned the conversation toward me and asked about the little boy inside of me.

I closed my eyes and said, "Yes, there was a little boy and he's behind the couch hiding."

John inquired, "Why is he hiding? What is he scared of?"

"I don't know; he feels alone," I replied. "No one is around. He feels safe behind the couch."

Then John brought Jesus into the scene: "Jesus is there and He wants to comfort you. Can you see Him?"

"I can, but I don't want to," I replied.

"What is Jesus doing?"

I said, "I can see Him, and He is reaching His hand out. But I said I can't go. I'm not sure I trust Him."

John said, "Ask Him if you can trust Him."

So I did. "Jesus, can I trust you?"

Jesus replied, "Yes, you can. I love you more than you'll ever know." He continued to reach His hand out and said to me, "You can come whenever you're ready." We sat for a while and Jesus stayed with me, patiently waiting for me to be ready. After a few minutes, it was like I started to come out from behind the couch and, in my mind, I crawled onto His lap as a little boy. He held me as if I were the only thing that mattered in the world. For the first time in my life, the little boy inside of me felt safe. I sat in the therapy session and just cried.

John then suggested that I ask Jesus where my pain was.

"Jesus, why am I so scared?" I asked. "What is wrong?"

Jesus replied, "You don't recognize my love for you. You don't feel loved here where you live."

I said, "I feel alone and scared."

"You can always turn to me and ask for my hand or ask me to hold you," Jesus assured me. "I will always be here for you no matter what, forever. I will never leave you." It stunned me that the conversation with Jesus was so clear.

I sat in John's office for quite a while, releasing the tears I had bottled up inside me for so long. The pain that was leaving me, the freedom that I felt, was something that I had never imagined or felt before.

When we finished this exercise, I felt like all of my emotions, all of my cards, all of my being, had been pulled out of me and laid out on the desk before me. It was all so raw. I've heard of different counseling methods where you slowly peel back your emotions, one layer at a time, and hopefully you eventually discover a core where your pain resides. Somehow John was able to lead me to reach out to Jesus Christ and trust Him, and He reached all the way into my heart and accessed the core of my pain in a matter of minutes.

During the week of the program, we encountered several topics and issues that both Roxane and I had to work through. At one point we came to the topic of infidelity. I had already told Roxane about my affair and the prostitutes, but I had never thought to mention Kelly. After all, she was not a real person but someone I had made up in my mind; I didn't even consider that my "imaginary friend" could affect or have an impact on our relationship.

During my discussions with John, we got on the subject of other places my heart had been and that's when Kelly came up. I told him about how I had created her back when I was probably in the first grade and how she had just been with me and evolved throughout my life. By this time, I had kept her alive in my mind for around thirty years.

Upon learning about Kelly, John told me that he had been a little confused through the first several days of our counseling because the level, depth, and duration of my emotional pain didn't seem to match the outcome for me. He didn't understand why I was not in a deep depression or why my sexual actions were not even worse than they were. But now he realized that some of my needs were being met through Kelly—she had kept me from completely falling out of reality. He also explained that it is with Kelly where my heart truly resides. It was just like having an affair, since my emotional connection was with Kelly and not Roxane. I'd never even considered this possibility. John also suggested that Kelly may have kept me from growing and maturing emotionally, and her stronghold on me may be what was keeping me from God, because Kelly was stronger and meant more to me than God. John even said that he suspected there was some type of demonic relationship with Kelly. She wasn't simply a thought that I had created to fill a need. Rather, he suggested, at my time of need as a six- or seven-year-old, something took control of my heart and was keeping it from ever connecting in a true way with God. Although this sounded a little out there to me, at this point I was willing to do anything to free myself of the burden and the chains that had held me back for most of my life. John said some special prayers and then told me that I needed to prayer and, through my prayers, to essentially divorce Kelly from my heart.

This special week of spiritual counseling was life changing for both me and Roxane. However, I would find in the years to come that there was much more on an even deeper level that was still controlling my behavior. Even with therapy, I had not healed or even recognized the huge emotional damage I had suffered in my heart. The topic of addiction never did come up in the sessions with John.

Even though this week had a profound impact on both of us, we found that John had spent much more time on me than on Roxane. As a result, we would later discover that Roxane still carried a lot of pain from her childhood in addition to the wounds that I had inflicted on her.

# Chapter 12

## The Struggle to Heal and Grow

At the end of our week of intensive therapy, we went back home, our emotions raw. It felt like somebody had opened our hearts and, with an ice-cream scoop, just dug and dug; though a lot of negative stuff had been removed, the wound was left open and raw. I had a strange feeling that various spiritual presences were around me. Mostly I felt the Holy Spirit and Christ, but I could feel other presences as well. Even though I always believed in God, I had never really formed a relationship or reached out to Him. The insightful letter I received from Jesus at the retreat a few years ago was now a hazy memory; it seemed surreal. But this time, something was different.

That first night back, I awoke at about 2 a.m. with a sense that this overpowering evil was in our bedroom. I woke up Roxane and told her about it. Although she didn't feel it herself, the fact that I did was kind of freaking her out. She thought I was losing my mind and so did I. But I couldn't deny it—it felt as if there were demons in the room and that they were pissed off about where I had gone and the relationship I had started with

Christ. Roxane was so disturbed by what I was describing that she actually called one of our close friends in the middle of the night to tell them what was going on. They prayed with us over the phone, asking for Jesus to remove all evil in His name. I felt the presences back off a bit after this, but I could still feel that they were there, though now were powerless. After a few hours I was able to fall back asleep, and when I got up in the morning, the feelings were gone. They never did come back. To this day, I don't know if they were real, if I was actually sensing something, or if my emotions were so raw that my mind was simply running wild.

During my spiritual growth, along with my conversion to the Catholic faith, I had come to learn and accept what we call spiritual warfare. That is, that there is a true, behind-the-scenes war between Satan and God for our souls. I think that many of the negative thoughts and fears that we experience are not placed by God but by Satan. Feelings of fear are not something God provides. I think there are hundreds of times in Scripture where God and Jesus both would say fear not and then continue to say something else of importance.

I've come to believe that any emotion of fear in my life was an influence of Satan, where his evil presence or whatever I may believe tried to pull me away from God and His true desire for me. When a person feels fear, it instills feelings of abandonment and being alone, and causes them to resist moving forward with what they know is right and just. It causes us to be self-centered and selfish and to see only our own needs. What I have learned is that this relates to pride, which is itself a centered act of focusing on oneself rather than outside of oneself. In this, Satan's ultimate goal is to make us focused on ourselves so we can't hear the words and desires of God.

For our continued healing and growth with each other, John had given Roxane and me an assignment. Each day, we were supposed to speak to each other's heart, saying how we felt about the other person, how we cherish them, and how we always wanted to be there for them. John told us this homework would be critical in continuing the heartfelt growth we had begun during the week of counseling. During that week in John's office, Roxane and I discovered within each other the pain of the child that we had both hid inside, which would in turn cause the behavior that we did not like. For example, if Roxane would get frustrated or feel rejected for some reason, she would shut down emotionally and tend to respond with anger. Through our counseling, I learned to see that this behavior was actually that of a small child who was feeling rejected and hurt; she was responding with anger to protect herself from further pain. This insight helped me avoid responding to my angry spouse and instead to have compassion for the child who was revealing her emotional pain. In this way, we both learned a much better way of reacting to each other and our negative behavior, because we could see what was causing it from the inside.

Roxane and I did make a point of doing this homework for a few weeks, and then life kind of set in, we got busy, and we let it slip by the wayside. As a result, we slowly returned to our old ways of interacting; we no longer stopped and saw the child within when the other person reacted in a certain way, but instead started reacting ourselves and so began fighting more. Within about six months, because we had failed to make our recovery work a priority, we were back to the way we were before the intensive counseling. Our life went on as it had before—we seemed to just be roommates who had very little emotional interaction or connection. I know this occurred because we failed to do the necessary work with ourselves.

For the next several months, we had our usual ups and downs, though sometimes emotions related to my affair and other infidelities would surface and Roxane would experience lots of anger. When she had that anger, she would verbally attack me and I would go on the defense, as if I were being attacked—when in reality I should have been responding to the person inside whom I had hurt; I should have had compassion for the wounds that I caused. But I didn't want to address what I had done and go there because of my own emotional distress, so I just got angry and let myself feel that I was being attacked. This response, in turn, usually made Roxane feel further betrayed, as if I had never expressed sorrow or had remorse for my actions. Yet this was actually far from the truth. I felt horrible about my affair and other infidelities—I was just unable to respond emotionally in a way that she was expecting. I just couldn't get it out. I had so much pain and insecurities myself that I couldn't go there and expose my feelings in a way that would express the sorrow that she needed to see. In fact, seeing how my behavior had affected and caused pain for her only served to increase my feelings of inadequacy and worthlessness, thus making it even harder for me to express my emotions and sorrow.

# Chapter 13

## Marked Men

A few years later a friend of mine exposed me to an organization called Marked Men for Christ. The group organized weekend retreats for men that featured various activities designed to help men access and then heal their inner pain.

I chose to attend one of these retreats to try to learn more about myself. The experience was very positive and brought out new things in addition to what I had uncovered with the biblical counseling a few years before. These weekend retreats are designed to go much deeper than the one I attended immediately after the affair. Because the details of how this particular program works is proprietary, I am unable to share too much. I can only say it is a very powerful experience and I recommend it to any man, regardless of where you are in your journey. (Details of the program are in the Resources section of this book.)

After the retreat weekend, the attendees are assigned to a local group for follow up and additional personal work. These groups of men meet every week or so. During the meetings, we work through various exercises that stir up emotions and thoughts about our pasts that may have fueled our current behaviors. I remember an exercise at one meeting where we were instructed to draw our dinner table from when we were around age ten and then write the names of the people who sat around our table and where they sat. Next we were asked to write some notes on what we remembered of our experience at the dinner table—was there talking, was it loud or silent, did our father interrogate us about our school and grades, was there arguing with our parents, and so on.

After the exercise, we went around the circle and shared our experience and what we remembered. When my turn came, I had nothing, absolutely nothing. I found it surprising, but I could not even remember sitting at a dinner table any time in my childhood, not even for holidays. As I thought more about this and tried to dig up some details from my childhood, I couldn't even remember eating. This began to disturb me. *Why couldn't I remember anything about eating or being with my family for meals?*

In the following months, I would occasionally think about my childhood and what I could remember. I was realizing more and more that I remembered extremely little. I would remember some things about school, such as classes, friends, and band concerts, but nothing about my home. Over the following few years, from time to time I would just think back on my life to see what I could recall. I became progressively disturbed at the holes in my memories, especially concerning my younger years. Yet even this did not seem clear cut; I found it especially strange that I had a ton of memories about being in college, but virtually none from the time I spent at home during those years. I could write volumes and volumes on my experiences with college friends, teachers, classes, roommates, and so on, but I couldn't even remember going home for the summer. I knew I must have spent my summers at home, because there's nothing else I would have done or nowhere else I would have gone, but I couldn't remember being there; it was as if it were blacked out from my mind. I started to wonder if something bad had happened to me a young age at home, but I couldn't recall anything. At one point, I even asked my mom about my childhood and commented that my memories were very limited. She started asking me about different things that had happened and if I remembered them. Each time I replied no. Eventually, she just said, "Well, I guess everybody remembers things differently." And that was that— no insight, no other thoughts, no nothing. That was obviously a dead end to find out anything about my early years. I'll get to more about this later.

# Chapter 14
## The Relapse

It was roughly eight years after my affair and it seemed like things with Roxane had slid back to where they were at the beginning of our marriage. There was very little intimacy, and she seemed to resent everything I did. In short, she was still angry and in pain over what had happened. Time had moved on, even though we never completely dealt with my sexual indiscretions. And now it was starting again. I had gradually fallen back into viewing pornography and acting out. In the recent years and months, it had become more and more frequent. To this point I had been able to withstand going any further than this, but then one day I was out doing some business errands and drove by a massage parlor I had seen multiple times before. For whatever reason, I decided to stop by this time and go in. Let's just say that I experienced a little more than a massage. Afterward, I felt so disgusted with myself, a change from how I used to feel after this type of sexual acting out. This time, I somehow recognized that my behavior wasn't actually about sex; rather, it was more about trying to fill a void in my life—a void that could not be filled by this activity. I felt so horrible that I drove immediately to our church, looking for a priest to hear my confession. I knew I had to do this right now or I wouldn't follow through. I was in a panic. No one was available at our usual church, so I started driving from church to church until I found a priest who could listen to my confession. After I'd finished, I told myself I can't do this again. Unfortunately, I had no idea of what was to come.

Several months later, Roxane told me she had some irritation near her genitals and thought it was probably a yeast infection. She tried to treat it with over-the-counter creams with no success. She eventually decided to go to the doctor to have it checked out; there she was tested and found to have a sexually transmitted disease. It wasn't anything fatal, but it was evidence that I had strayed from our marriage yet again. She became completely unglued, and this time she was talking divorce. All at once, my whole world began collapsing around me. I was so shaken that my heart started racing and I felt short of breath. I actually went to the hospital, fearing that I was having a heart attack. They did tests and admitted me for a couple of days for observation but in the end found nothing. They chalked it up to a panic attack. That was an understatement. If nothing else, the couple of days I spent away in the hospital gave Roxane time to calm down; now she was only completely pissed off rather than ready to kill me and walk out. I knew she was completely justified in every emotion she had. What I couldn't believe was that I had done this again. What was going on—why did I mess up and act out again; why does this behavior seem to have a force of its own that I can't control? I couldn't answer any of it. Yet I finally started to realize that maybe, I have a problem.

In the coming weeks, Roxane shared my latest betrayal with most of our close friends, who all encouraged her to work things out and for both of us to seek professional help. They suggested that our first step might be to visit Father Ken Leone. Father Ken was the one who, eight years ago, handed me the letter at the retreat that was signed by Jesus. In the years after receiving the letter that spoke to my heart, I had come to know Father Ken a little and discovered that he had a very special connection with God. He was the perfect person for us to see.

Roxane and I agreed to give counseling with Father Ken a try. Before we went to meet with him, I decided on my own to do a little research on the Internet about sexual addiction. It was something that had crossed my mind before, but I had always dismissed it or denied it as a possibility. I would think, "I'm not one of those people. Addicts are those creepy people who sell drugs to buy sex; I'm not like that!" Little did I know that without the Grace of God to this point in my life, I could be in that very situation.

I found a website with a questionnaire that would rate the likelihood that I was a sex addict. I went through the test, answering dozens of questions, and the tally of my responses gave me a score of 15 out of a possible 16. The higher the score, the more likely it is that you are a sex addict. It seemed that pedophilia or sex with children and homosexuality were the only areas I didn't have a problem in. Between the score on the assessment and the STD I gave my wife, I had finally hit my lowest point, what some in recovery circles call their "bottom." I said to myself, "Well this kind of confirms it then; I don't really have an option but to face this and do something about it." Denial was no longer an option; I was about to lose everything, maybe I already had. A few years ago I would not have been able to accept this diagnosis. But with my life in shambles, I knew it was time to admit it and move forward.

My secret was out now, and I was aware of the impact of my behavior. It was no longer an alternate life or a different reality. I couldn't live like it was anymore. Acting out was much more a "conscious" behavior now, and I knew that I couldn't control it. I had never really faced it before. Even with the biblical counseling, we never recognized the addiction or addressed anything at that level. All of the attempts I made in the past to set things right had failed, because the underlying problems that caused my behavior always crept back in eventually.

## Addict to Addict

Have you ever said to yourself, "I can beat this," only to fail time and time again? You don't want to admit that there's something stronger and more powerful than you; doing so would only make you feel more powerless and worthless than you already do. "No way will I ever be defeated" you say to yourself. The hard reality is that "you" can't beat this; "you" can't control this. But it can be beaten. Am I talking in circles? Absolutely not, keep reading.

My back was against the wall; I really had no other options. I did not tell Roxane that I took the test or what I scored at the time; I just needed to know for myself. Before we met with Father Ken, I did share with her that I thought I may have an addiction problem. She was not happy to hear that; she responded, "Oh great, so I'm married to a sex addict—what a waste of my life."

Fortunately, in a few days we met with Father Ken, and he did a great job of calming us down and helping us to see what we needed to do to move forward. One of the critical things he said was that I had to seek help for the addiction. Knowing my history, he agreed that there was a strong possibility I was a sex addict. Father Ken told me about a group of men that met at his church one evening a week to work on issues such as mine.

Called Romans 6, this group was made up of sex addicts who got together to share their experiences, their struggles, and their lives. He said that they used various study aids and workbooks to learn about and work through their addictions, and he gave me a list of some materials that I should get before attending my first meeting. The first was a workbook called *Facing the Shadows* by Patrick Carnes, which was a guide to starting sexual and relationship recovery for people with sexual addiction. The second was an audio CD set by Christopher West called *Winning the Battle for Sexual Purity*. With this CD, I would be finally introduced to what sex was really about; I would learn about the "theology of the body" teachings of the church and about God's plan for sexuality as well as Satan's efforts to derail it.

# Recovery

# Chapter 15

## Romans 6: Finding True Recovery

*In the same way, you must see yourselves as being dead to sin but alive for God in Christ Jesus.*

*That is why you must not allow sin to reign over your mortal bodies and make you obey their desires;*

*or give any parts of your bodies over to sin to be used as instruments of evil. Instead, give yourselves to God, as people brought to life from the dead, and give every part of your bodies to God to be instruments of uprightness;*

*and then sin will no longer have any power over you—you are living not under law, but under grace.*

—Romans 6:11–14

The next week I went to my first Romans 6 meeting, which would become the place where my real healing began. This addiction group was not run or even supervised by a trained counselor, but by other recovering addicts who have made significant discoveries, progress, and enlightenment about themselves. I knew the guy who headed up the group; we had met years before at the first men's retreat I attended. His name was Desi. Desi welcomed me into the group and introduced me to the other members

The group meeting started and followed a certain protocol. First, we all gathered in a circle, held hands, and said a prayer of confidentiality—a statement reminding us that what is said here stays here and that our efforts are to create a safe environment so everyone feels comfortable sharing whatever is on their heart without fear of judgment. The next couple of phases were check-in rounds. In the first round, we went around the circle and shared what our feelings were at that moment or for the day, describing the feeling in a sentence or two. The second round was the accountability round. This is where we took turns basically reporting on how the last week went with regards to our addiction and acting out. I was amazed at how candid and upfront everybody was in their struggle as well as their failures. I definitely felt as if I had found a home; for the first time I had a safe place where I could speak freely of my failures and how I felt about them. I had never imagined there would be anywhere I could feel so comfortable. It was as if the weight of this tremendous secret and alternate reality of life was lifted from my shoulders. During my first meeting, the group took time out of the usual routine and the existing group members each gave a five-minute talk about their lives and about becoming a sex addict. Again, as each man shared, I felt more and more comfortable with the idea of being honest about what I felt and sharing my own story. I related to the stories of the other men in the group; some had acted out less than me, some more than my history revealed. I would eventually find that it was in the sharing with others in this safe, nonjudgmental environment where the true healing took place. Here you could actually share all of the deep, dark, and dirty secrets that no one else ever knew and you had thought you could never tell anybody—and everyone understood. No judgment! They understood the pain. I never thought this was even possible. But the feeling of knowing that I wasn't alone was more than I can even explain. It was the right place for me to be.

## Addict to Addict

As a struggling addict, I would always have feelings of loneliness, emptiness, helplessness, guilt, worthlessness, and general feelings like I wanted to walk away from everything. *This is just too hard to fight and nobody understands me. I can't even let my wife see this side of me. I feel like I'm actually living two different lives*, I thought. But then I discovered the Romans 6 group and learned that I wasn't alone after all. You're not alone either. Others can understand what you've been through because they've been through the same thing. Seek out help. You don't have to do this alone. Talk to your clergyperson, a counselor, or look on the Internet for groups in your area that may be the right fit for you.

The next part of the meeting was an open time in which group members could share or discuss anything that was on their minds. To my surprise, one man shared that he had been having an affair and his wife had just found out. He said he wasn't going to be in the group for the next few weeks, as he and his wife were both going to an intensive therapy center out of state to work on his addiction and their recovery. What this man had to say hit me hard. Tears actually collected in my eyes as I felt his pain. I wished there were something I could do for him in his time of need. I knew that time would heal and his life would move on, but at the moment he seemed hopeless and with no direction. Nobody else seemed to have anything to say in response to his news other than that they would pray for him. While that was well and good, I felt that this man needed some words of encouragement as he faced his addiction. He needed to know that there is a future and things will get better. But no one said that. This weighed heavily on my heart, and I have since felt the call to reach out to others with the same struggles. It's almost selfish in a way because I find that as I help or talk to others about this topic, I feel stronger myself.

Desi said they normally work out of the Patrick Carnes book, but for the last few weeks they had been listening to and discussing the Christopher West audio talk. I was excited to hear this because I had just ordered these materials and was already anxious to listen to them. In the group that night they played the third disc from the CD set. The audio included a tremendous amount of insight that helped me see deeper within my addiction. Christopher West had a unique way of speaking about sexuality so that you see God's plan and the holiness for which sex was intended.

I left the meeting with the sense that in this community of men, I could finally come clean and admit my addiction, my failures, and my pain. All without judgment but with compassion. And when I say compassion, I don't mean permission. While it's clear to many people that sexual addiction is a serious problem, in the group I met with others who were in the same boat, and they all really "got it" and know how hard it is to battle and recover from.

At times when I told others about this program, they asked me if it was a type of Twelve Step program. The first time I was asked this, I had never even heard of such a program and had no idea what they were. After being asked this several times over several months, I decided to look up what this Twelve Step thing was. As I read over the steps, I realized that while Romans 6 wasn't based on a Twelve Step program—it's more free-form—it nonetheless informally covers most of what's in the Twelve Steps. Some areas, mainly the spirituality part, are more intense in Romans 6 than what they seem to be in the Twelve Step program (this is my assumption from reading about them; I have never taken part in any such program). Other areas of the Twelve Steps seem to be evident in Romans 6, but they're not specifically done in any type of steps. They just kind of happen in the course of what we do.

At the next week's Romans 6 meeting, I discovered that one of the members, Bob, had been trying to find somewhere to start a second group on the north side of Denver. This group currently met on the south side and was nearly an hour's drive in traffic for me. While I was willing to make the drive, a location closer to me was definitely attractive. I asked Desi if I could join Bob and the north group. Desi said yes, definitely, especially since Bob was currently the only member of this new group and he obviously needed someone else to join him to get it going.

I would later find out that this was all in God's plan for me.

I continued to attend Romans 6 meetings, and in time I could feel myself begin to change. As I spent more time with other addicts talking about our deeper problems and issues, healing began. Roxane and others could see the changes in me as well. The trust in our relationship started to come back, and this time it didn't seem like it was only complacency with time. She could really see the difference. Today, Roxane is still cautious and at times gets attacked herself with old thoughts sparking anger and old pain, but I guess I seem to be more compassionate and sorry than before.

Sometimes little things will spark old stuff. One time

recently, two years after Romans 6 started, I was in a car accident and afterward had to undergo physical therapy on my upper back and neck. The physical therapist suggested that I get a massage. The mere suggestion sparked a little anxiety in me, and I casually asked the therapist, "How do I know one is legit? Many out there offer extras." He knew what I meant. He said that if they are partnered with a chiropractor or acupuncture medical office, they should be fine. So I found one close to home and went. It was good and helped my injury. They of course took my personal information for the medical file and the HIPPA regulations. The problem was that almost a year later, I got an email offering a massage special. Roxane was browsing through my email and flipped out. "Where have you gone, what is this place, and why do they have your info? You must have been there—what have you been doing?" she asked. I didn't remember the name of the place, I didn't know who they were, and I honestly couldn't remember any association with them. She was mad, thinking that it was happening again. I couldn't sleep that night, worried about what this was. I knew that any massage parlors I had been to in the past didn't take personal information, so who were these people? At 4 a.m. I finally got up, looked up the address for the place, and drove to it. Once I saw the building, I recognized it and remembered the therapy. I went home, woke up Roxane, and told her. She wasn't even really awake but still seemed relieved. So even after trust is mostly rebuilt, there is still a "heightened sense of awareness" and the pain and memories remain right under the surface and can easily be touched. I suspect that it will always be that way and that's fine by me. I can't expect anything different. And if I'm clean, it shouldn't matter.

# Chapter 16

## The Desperate Search for God

Meanwhile I received the CD set by Christopher West that I had ordered. I decided to set aside one morning in my office on a Saturday when no one was around to play the first CD. I started listening to the CD and was pleasantly impressed with what I heard. Mr. West had a very clear and concise way of speaking about sexuality within God's plan. During the presentation, Christopher came to a part where he quoted G. K. Chesterton. The quote went like this:

*Every man who knocks on the door of a brothel is looking for God.*

Wow—this hit me like a ton of bricks; I had to pause the CD. It was like I had been kicked in the side of the head; I felt this message to my core. I began to weep uncontrollably. All of a sudden I knew: God was exactly what I had been looking for. Every time I had ever acted out, every time I visited a prostitute, and every time I went to a massage parlor or even looked at pornography, I was in a desperate search for God.

It was the right time for me to hear this and to comprehend it. On paper, making the statement that when you act out sexually, it is actually an attempt to find God sounds ludicrous. As illogical as it sounds, I knew it was true. At this point and place in my life, I understood that it really was unconditional love and acceptance that I was seeking every time I acted on my sexual impulses or desires. And, yes, I was looking for God. I wanted someone to tell me I was good enough and to accept me—even if I had to pay for it. The absurdity of it all reveals the power of addiction and how strong its grip was on me.

I continued to play the CD and slowly began to understand the premise and confusion behind my sexual addiction. He spoke about how the world has taught us that these perverted acts we perform are love, when in fact they are what he called a counterfeit for love. But since the world tells us this, we continue to seek it because we are looking for love. We do it over and over again and every time come up short—because a counterfeit is not the real deal. In fact, it is trash. It's like eating from a dumpster without knowing it because we have never experienced anything different. He went on to talk about sex as God designed it. Christopher said that Pope John Paul II in his theology of the body writings said, "Purity is the glory of the human body before God."

He also said that the true desire for sex is the desire to be joined as one, as God designed us to be. God created us, male and female, to be joined as one as a form of life-giving love and communion. Any act performed outside of love and marriage is a perversion of God's plan. Scripture says, "A man shall leave his father and mother in be united with his wife and they shall become one." It's the evil ways of the world that have handed us pornography and prostitution as a substitute for what God desires. Again, this is like eating from the dumpster when we can be eating from a five-star restaurant for free.

All of the pornography, prostitution, masturbation, and so on in today's world are counterfeit forms of love. Our culture has taught us that such distortions are real, but since that is a lie, we are never satisfied. Instead, we feel empty and sick inside just as if we really ate out of a dumpster. *"But the problem is that we don't know any better!"*

Christopher talked about how Satan cannot make up anything new; he can only take the truth that God has given, twist it, pervert it, and present it as the truth. And this is precisely how the beautiful God-created act of sex became twisted into lust and pornography.

I've also since learned the truth that sex is Satan's number one weapon on men. It's dark and scary but the most powerful and most prevalent addiction there is. And most people don't know what it means to be a sex addict. It's taboo. You can tell someone you're a recovering alcoholic, and they may say, "Oh, I understand. Good for you." But if you tell them you're a recovering sex addict, they gather their children and run! You're looked upon as the beast that will devour them. And maybe they have the right insight but for reasons they don't even realize. The beast (Satan) is the one who turned God's beautiful plan for sexuality into the twisted, perverted, dark plan that it is today in this world, and really always has been. Sex with your spouse is God's plan; indeed, the euphoric experience of two joined together as one is the closest physical experience to God that we will ever have until we reach heaven. Anything outside of this is a severe abuse of God's will and plan, which is why it is of such interest to Satan. It's the most powerful weapon he has, in essence the biggest "up yours" weapon he has against God to prevent God's design of creation and procreation. God creates, but Satan can only destroy.

# Addict to Addict

Do you ever wonder what's wrong with you? The answer is nothing. You are doing exactly what you were created to do. You are following the natural instinct that God put in us. God created us to love. He created us to procreate, to have children in His image. God created us so that when we are aroused or attracted to a woman, a chemical called dopamine is released in the brain. This dopamine is a naturally created drug that gives us pleasure and a kind of "high" or "excitement." It is designed to make our relationship with our spouse more pleasurable and rewarding. It thus creates the urge to make love, to join and create life—life in God's image. Because we are flawed human beings with a wounded soul, Satan takes this opening to feed his lies. Take this natural act, twist it, and be trained by this world's immoral ways to chase that "high" or euphoric feeling anywhere and with anyone, and we change this God-created purpose to an immoral act that disrupts God's plan. Combine this with the childhood wounds; the negative self-image; the pain and feelings of rejection, worthlessness, and self-loathing; and outright craving for love and acceptance that we addicts have, and now you have a cocktail for disaster. It's a completely destructive downward spiral that only gets worse, and the more you fight it, the more power it has over you. In the end, you're left with a feeling of complete helplessness. But here's the kicker, there is a way out! Read on.

The rest of the Christopher West CD series included so much thought-provoking material that I had to listen to it at least three times just to begin to absorb what he had to say. It was a radical, life-changing way to look at what I had been struggling with my entire life: the way sex is supposed to be according to God's plan; why we behave the way we do. While it didn't change my situation or behavior immediately, I was much more aware of what I was doing and how I was responding to thoughts of any type of lustful act, pornography, or even the idea of masturbation.

# Chapter 17
## Romans 6, Phase 2

I was now attending meetings at the new Romans 6 group that had formed up north closer to my home. For the first several weeks, Bob and I were the only men at these meetings. This actually turned out to be wonderful gift, as he and I connected deeply and had an uncanny set of similarities in our lives and experiences. Bob had been attending Romans 6 meetings for a couple of years by the time I joined, so he had a tremendous amount of history and healing to share with me.

One thing I'll never forget is what Bob casually shared during the check-in of one of our early meetings. He described how when he would have a conversation with a woman who was attractive and who was being kind to him, his mind would instantly leap and start thinking about that person as a potential partner—not just in a sexual way but also in an emotional way. His vision of this person would lead to thinking, "If only they loved me, then everything would be okay; my life would then be fine." While he was saying that, I had to interrupt him: "Holy crap! I do the same thing, but I didn't even realize it!" We then began to talk about these types of thoughts and how we each have them. Bob said they were part of his early warning system: when he began to have such thoughts about a person, he knew they would trigger inappropriate behavior. And he knew that he needed to stop those thoughts right then. I was amazed that this was something I did frequently—having these thoughts after just seeing another person or having a conversation with them—but I didn't even realize what these thoughts were really about, nor did I realize how dangerous they were and the downhill slide they actually started. It had never occurred to me.

For the next week after our meeting, I began to catch myself having such thoughts every time I saw an attractive woman or had a pleasant conversation with one at any business I worked with or bank or grocery store I walked into. It was as if anytime a woman would give me the time of day, my mind would jump to "Maybe she likes me and if she likes me, then maybe she would want me and then I would be okay." These thoughts could be purely emotional to start, but they could easily turn sexual. I realized that I was so desperate to be accepted and loved that I would even create short fantasies about complete strangers, and I discovered that I was doing this ten or twenty times a day! It floored me how often this happened. And what's more, I never saw it before. I began to catch myself having these thoughts almost continuously, even when seeing a car passing by with an attractive woman in it. This obviously was a problem. However, now I could at least see what was happening, and I hoped that would help me stop myself before these fantasies got started. I realized that in the past, such thoughts would lead to sexual thoughts and thus the desire to act out physically. And then it all clicked in my mind—I suddenly understood why all of what I had called "silly little actions" such as blocking certain programs on TV or blocking certain things on the Internet wasn't going to solve anything. While they are single, small, and required steps, they have very minimal effect in battling these thoughts. This was partly because I knew I could find the images elsewhere if I really wanted to, but mostly because so much of what started the "train moving down the tracks" so to speak just existed in everyday life, and you can't stop that. While I understand that having blocks on TV and Internet may do some good and should be done—these images do serve as a catalyst for more thoughts—in the larger scheme of things, they are minimally effective. The real problem is me and why these images have the effect they do.

In the coming weeks other men began attending the Romans 6 program; some stayed, some didn't. I always found it disturbing when someone didn't come back. I always felt like somehow we had failed them, that they needed something and we didn't provide it. Bob explained that when he started the north group, Desi told him that during the ten years he had been doing Romans 6 meetings, many men would come to a few meetings but very few stayed. It seemed likely that when someone came into the group for the first time and experienced the depth of honesty and sharing that took place, they would feel uncomfortable if they weren't yet ready for that level of sharing. And it's true—it is very difficult to open up in such a way around strangers. Sexual addiction is a very dark and personal disease.

## Addict to Addict

The struggle to overcome or heal from sex addiction is difficult and very real. I think one of the most difficult things about being a sex addict is accepting how challenging this battle really is. And when you're on the front lines of the battle, it can be frustrating and demoralizing to hear from the general public that it's not really an addiction. I remember when the scandal about Tiger Woods came out, and there was constant talk on the radio from supposedly educated people who would just say: "Why doesn't he just *not* do it?" Such comments really go a long way toward making sex addicts feel that their struggles are not valid and shouldn't even exist. This makes this addiction that much more embarrassing and shameful. It just adds to the thoughts of "If anyone ever really knew what I did, they would never understand and I would be completely rejected." We can pray that someday sex addiction will be looked upon like alcoholism once was. It wasn't all that long ago that alcoholism was viewed only as a moral weakness, but now it is recognized by the American Medical Association (AMA) as a true disease.

---

One other member who came to the group meetings for several months was Mike. He was very knowledgeable about Scripture and various writings in the church. Plus, he had a lot of other useful insights that I found very helpful in my struggles. There was one significant thing he told me that led to the prayer that I now say on a daily basis. I had shared that I was having difficulty giving up control over my addiction, the idea that I alone could not stop it. By the time we joined Romans 6, we had all come to accept that we could not cure this illness by ourselves. This was not something we could do alone. Mike asked me, "Do have the desire to release control to God over your addiction?" I told him honestly that I didn't know if I was ready to give it up or not. He then asked, "Do you desire the desire to give it up?" I said, "Yes, I desire the desire to give up control." He said that is all that God wants; He can work with that. Even if we don't have the desire itself, He can work with us as long as we want that desire. I knew I was afraid to let go of the addiction because it was so much a part of me and who I was. It was my comfort and medication when I was feeling low, rejected, alone, etc., which was the majority of the time. Although it was a dirty and perverted part, it was nonetheless part of my identity, who I was, and I was afraid that if I really gave it up, I would lose who I am. This was kind of a sick thought, but it's where I was.

Yet I was so tired of running my own life now; it would be so much smoother, more joyful if I allowed God to run it. I felt like there was a battle inside to retain control. I knew what it was and I just wanted to give in and let Him take over everything, but I just couldn't quite let go. I was so tired. I was almost ready to give it all over to Him. It was just too hard to hold on to anymore.

After this conversation with Mike at the last meeting, I was inspired and came up with the following prayer that, even today, I say on a daily basis:

*Dear Lord Jesus Christ, I desire the desire to surrender my heart and my entire being to you but I cannot do it; I fear the abandonment of losing control of who I am. I ask that you take what little space I can open to you, use it, and invade my heart, take it captive, and protect it from all evil. I beg for your help in my complete surrender to you.*

Little did I know that God was listening. I had no idea that this prayer would eventually be answered and in ways I could never have imagined.

One of the things that I came to believe, which has been told to me by others on many occasions, is that when you pray, God will answer your prayers. This is especially true if you do your best to ask God for His will for you. While I didn't realize it at the time, my prayer was actually a "surrender prayer." I was praying to God about my desire to surrender to Him, and it seemed appropriate to acknowledge my faults and the roadblocks that were preventing me from doing just that. I think the very thing that God wants us to do is to completely hand our lives over to Him and to live out His will. For me, the question about the meaning of life that other people seem to struggle with is very simple. The meaning of life is to know, to love, and to serve God. And when we do that, He will bless us abundantly in our hearts. These blessing will not always be treasures in this world; rather, He will bring us such peace that we can have it no other way. And while I didn't understand it at the time, my begging Him to take what little space I could give Him and come into my heart was precisely what He asks of all of us. By opening myself up to desiring His will, He answered just that.

Through different events in my life, but mostly when meeting with my Romans 6 group, I began to learn a lot more about myself and about why I do the things that I do. For so long I had been focused on trying to find a reason for what was wrong with me—what could have happened during my childhood to cause this? I was looking for that smoking gun, so to speak, of why I was so screwed up. Yet as hard as I looked, I couldn't find the answer. My memories of childhood were so sparse that I couldn't put together anything significant. It was just more of the same experience I had back when I tried to draw my childhood dinner table and where I sat at it—I couldn't remember the table or eating, period. The more I searched, the more frustrated I became with my inability to remember.

But now I was seeing the futility of my previous efforts; not only had I been searching in the wrong place for answers—I had been searching for the wrong answers. Instead of examining the dark recesses of my brain for memories that might tell me why I had a problem, I turned my attention to what really mattered: how to fill the emptiness in my soul. And, indeed, I was beginning to see that this emptiness could be filled by God and His love. Unfortunately, even though I understood this intellectually in my head, it hadn't yet sunk into my heart. After nearly a year of going to the Romans 6 group, I grew frustrated with myself. Although I was continuing to learn so much about myself and who I am, as well as my needs, it didn't seem as if I was battling my addiction any better. The information I was learning wasn't helping. I was still trying to manage the problem by myself, using my new knowledge to take more control over my addiction. My thinking went something like this: *Now that I understand what was going on, I should be able to control it, right?* My own thinking and reality were still worlds apart, as I had these thoughts at the same time that I was feeling less and less in control. From a mental perspective, I was actually getting worse. Every mildly attractive woman that I saw would still trigger thoughts that quickly turned sexual. And though I now had the tools to recognize that my thoughts were starting, it only made it more apparent that I couldn't stop them—they owned me; I had no control. These thought were taking over my life and rendering me unable to function. Even though my thoughts were not leading me to physically act out with someone, I was still out of control and I knew it. It owned me, and knowing it was the worst part. I knew it was only a matter of time before I would physically act out again, maybe even with someone. This thought terrified me, especially because I couldn't stop it.

Finally, one early morning when I was alone at my office, I hesitated before praying as I usually would. I felt like I was at my wit's end—I was really frustrated with myself that I didn't seem to be getting anywhere with my recovery. After some time of sitting there that morning, I started my normal surrender prayer, but in the middle of it I began to break down. I was weeping out of pain and frustration over my lack of progress. The feelings of anger and rage over what I was going through were overwhelming. I was desperate and completely out of control. The thought of the story by C. S Lewis in the *Great Divorce* about the Lizard of Lust popped into my head. In the story, the Ghost was afraid to let the Angel kill the lizard for fear it would kill him. (See the appendix to read this story in full if you are not familiar with it.)

I understood what he meant by the ghost not wanting to give up the lizard—it was part of him, but like a cancer, it had to be removed; it couldn't be managed. I began to pray, almost like a begging to God, saying out loud:

*Lord Jesus Christ, I cannot fight this battle anymore; I'm done. I hand you the dragon to slay; I hand you the lizard to slay. I walk away; it's yours. I'm done. I can't do this anymore. It's not my battle anymore.*

At this moment, I felt that I truly surrendered the battle to Jesus Christ. It was like I emptied myself of the addiction. For the first time, I felt the addiction—the battle—"separate" from me. I gave it up and handed it to Him as if it were His battle and not mine. At that moment I felt a rush of warmth flooding my body and felt almost as if I were having an out-of-body experience. It was like a warm liquid was pouring over me, and I felt what I can only describe as complete peace that I believe is the grace of God filling my heart. It was filling the void and completely removing all desire and temptation and need for anything from the outside world. I had never experienced anything like this or even close to this before. I could feel the spirit of God completely encasing me with His love and grace. It was a place I didn't want to leave. Although it probably lasted only a few minutes, it felt like hours. When I came out, I had never felt so much peace or strength in my life. It wasn't my strength or my control and ability to defend myself against temptation or an outside force; it was something else. It was something from within that wasn't mine. I just sat there and cried, as I knew I was in the presence of God.

For a brief time, I felt like the need for any pleasure or fulfillment from the world had completely evaporated. I remember thinking that I must have seen an ever-so-slight glimpse of heaven for a short period of time. This all happened on that early Saturday morning and, though I remember thinking that it kind of ruined my day for being able to get any work done, I didn't care. It was as if nothing else in the world mattered right now. After being out of the experience for a few minutes, I wanted to go back but I couldn't get there. I think this was a pure gift—being able to surrender 100 percent of my life and my battle to Jesus Christ.

I want to make a point here for those who are currently in the place where I was only a few weeks before this event, as some people have been confused when I have told them about what happened. When I say I surrendered or gave up the battle, I don't mean that I *gave in* to the battle. They are two completely different positions. When I gave it up, there was no battle, no temptation to give in to. We all carry a cross of our sins, things we've done and some things that are put upon us that are simply part of our life. In this experience, it was as if I took part of my cross and gave it to Christ, thus making mine lighter and easier to carry.

Over the next several weeks, the experience remained in the forefront of my mind and it continues to be—in fact, it still drives me now. As time went on, I would kind of flow back and forth between the way I was and the way I knew I could be. On occasions in prayer, I would be able to get closer to this experience again, but I was not able to completely get there. I think this is because I have not been at that point of desperation again to completely surrender myself; at that level, it is so hard to do. But what changed my life was that I knew it was possible, that it's there, and that I had experienced this feeling at least once—the grace that filled the void that I had been always trying to fill. Today, things occasionally go back to the way they were, but this does not happen nearly as frequently as it used to. I still struggle, but now I understand that the struggle is all about my attempting to take control and fill the void that can only be filled with God's perfect love. It's still hard sometimes, especially when the cravings come, to go back to that place. Even now, I tend to take control and have the desire to fill the void myself with all of the wrong means. Sometimes when life isn't going so well, I feel entitled, as if I deserve the worldly pleasures. I am noticing that behaviors in other parts of my life tend to fill in the void when sexually acting out is avoided—behaviors like work, food indulgence, or shopping to reward myself. I need to be careful, as they are really part of the addiction and a sign that I have not completely surrendered my pain or worked through my wounds with Christ. This is perfect material for me to bring to my addiction counselor and my Romans 6 group.

As the months passed after this experience, I continued to grow little by little, and I began to see that there was still a part that I didn't understand. I spoke before about my experience of listening to Christopher West's audio and how he referred to "eating from the dumpster" because we didn't know any better. What I couldn't understand is why, since I have "eaten from the buffet of God" in my surrender experience, I would still choose to eat from the dumpster. How could I be so stupid? I know the difference. I've been there; I know which is better, so why do I still dumpster dive? This was really disturbing me. During the next weeks at the Romans 6 meetings, Bob and I were the only ones there, and so I began to tell him about this dilemma and the frustration that I had in detail. Bob sat back, looked up into the distance as if he was getting some type of message or inspiration, something I had seen him do from time to time in the middle of our sessions. Then he sat back up and said, "God is telling me the answer, but He is also telling me not to tell you. He said you need to figure it out on your own." Bob said he had never gotten this kind of message from God before. Usually, he gets inspirations of things to say, but he's never been told not to tell anybody something. He thought this was very strange and said that even though he had the answer, he didn't understand it himself but was confident that I would when I figured it out.

That was a little frustrating, but I trusted the message was from God and that it was the way it needed to be. I struggled with just what this answer could be for many weeks. Then one day when I was in the adoration chapel, it finally came to me: I was returning to my old ways, in effect stuffing myself with "dumpster food," because I was afraid to take down the walls around me and let true love in. My self-preservation mode caused me to take control when what I needed to do was surrender the feelings that were surfacing. Whenever something happened that would lead me to feel rejected or inadequate or not good enough, or when something simple happened, like an attractive woman being kind to me at the bank or store or somewhere around town, a certain area of my mind would automatically latch on to the desire to be loved and filled up somehow. But instead of reacting to the natural feeling by actually seeking love in a healthy way, for whatever reason my defense mechanisms would take over and I would construct emotional walls and then try to take control of the situation myself. In an effort to protect my heart from pain, I would block out any true love and instead seek instant gratification to fulfill my need for acceptance. Now this would mean anything from having a mere fantasy or thoughts of someone to using pornography or acting out or in some way that was much worse. Whatever the activity, it of course never succeeded in filling what I needed and generally only made me feel worse. Still, it was where I would go; it's where all addicts go—back to eating from the dumpster. Recognizing and stopping this cycle is the key.

What I needed to do was recognize when I started to experience these feelings of inadequacy in any shape or form and then consciously stop myself from going into control mode, thus seeking acceptance within this world. Instead, I needed to lower my emotional walls, become vulnerable, and ask Jesus to come into my heart. I needed to attempt to reach that surrender point where I could feel God's grace and love, because that's the only thing that would truly fill this hole and rid me of my feeling of rejection and inadequacy.

It was great to finally figure this out, but I knew that executing it would be a whole other story. It's one thing to recognize when you are feeling not good enough, even to recognize it before you begin to "tank," but it's a completely different thing to stop that automatic reaction and give up control, be vulnerable, and surrender your heart to God. It's the opposite of what my "gut" would tell me to do. I had to "un-learn" forty-plus years of ingrained behavior. Even though I would remember what it felt like from my actual experience, it was still difficult to do. After all, this was something that was intangible and difficult to get ahold of, while imagining or fantasizing about something that was real was much easier and more accessible and sometimes led to physical behavior. I knew that the fantasy—or worse— was not the way to go, but it was immediate; it was what I was used to; and even though the guilt followed, it would relieve the craving. Half of addiction is following habits. My new battle was about recognizing when these feelings happen and pushing away my innate desire or reaction to put up my walls and control my environment. I would find growth in these situations from releasing and surrendering and by becoming open to the vulnerability to allow the love of God into my heart and to actually go there and invite Him in. I know it's what I have to do, but it's so hard to do.

Another part of my battle was to avoid fantasizing whenever I saw a woman who was attractive or provocatively dressed. With practice, I would now at least catch myself when I was beginning to fantasize and be aware of my thoughts at that moment. I would try to recall my experience of surrendering the battle to Christ. You hear people talk about the cross we must carry; well, I realized that this addiction was a big part of my cross and I began to see the surrender as me handing my cross to Jesus and telling Him, "I can't carry this anymore—I give it to you to carry." Now when I begin to think the thoughts that I know will carry me down the slippery path toward acting out, I stop, hand my cross to Christ, and mentally walk away. When I do this, the temptation, and the impure thoughts that go with it, all go away. It's like there is no addiction at that moment. I've even considered approaching the provocatively dressed woman and asking her if she knows that by dressing that way, she leads men to look at her with inappropriate desires and that men will see her as a plaything rather than the valuable real person she is. I've never had the guts to actually do this, but maybe someday I will.

Over the next several months, my time in prayer became more and more frequent. I tried to pray the surrender and battle prayers each day. Unexpectedly, God began to make some changes in my life. I've never really "heard" God before as a verbal voice in my head or otherwise, but I was starting to get a strong sense inside that my heart knew it was God. I started to get a gentle but strong message of Him saying, "I'm going to ask you to do something for me soon." It was almost freaky because this thought was strange and new, but it wouldn't go away. At a future Romans 6 meeting, I mentioned it and someone kind of jokingly said, "Maybe He's going to ask you to write a book." I laughed at the idea and said, "Yeah right, I don't even read—like I'm going to write a book!" Sometime later it came up again, and I dismissed it again.

Several weeks later I decided that maybe I should seek a spiritual director. I thought that  someone in this role might be able to help me sort out this feeling that God was going to ask me to do something. I just couldn't get it; I didn't know what He wanted. Maybe I wasn't listening close enough. I visited a priest who directed a center that specializes in growth and direction. He interviewed me so he could determine who would be the right fit for me. Strangely, in talking with this priest, the book thing came up again. I told him that it couldn't be what God wanted of me, because I have no education or expertise in that area, and besides, I don't even like to read, how would I ever write a book? I finally mentioned the whole idea to my wife and to my surprise, she said, "Maybe you should write a book, or at least a blog or something." This blew me away. Of all the people who have been hurt by what I have done, the one who was hurt the most was actually open to the idea of me somehow being more public about the whole experience. I was certain that writing about my addiction in any way would bring up old wounds and be very painful for her and others. But she said, "If that's what God wants you to do, then you need to do it." I again dismissed the suggestion, since I had no idea what I would even write. Plus, who was I to try to help anyone else? I couldn't even help myself half the time. But this was the fourth time that the idea of writing a book came up. I know that if God wants you to do something, He will keep hitting you with it over and over until you finally see it. But this just didn't make sense to me. I figured it must be something else, so I decided to just leave it alone. "If this is what He wants," I thought, "He'll just have to hit me over the head with it again, because I don't even know if this idea is really from God anyway." As it turns out, that's all it took.

# Chapter 18

## Sharing My Story: The Book

I was in the middle of a back-and-forth email conversation with a close friend of mine about what God was asking of me. We had discussed the possibility that maybe He wanted me to be involved in a job around a ministry or something like that, maybe even out of state. I told my friend that Roxane would never go for moving. I brought up the book thing that kept popping up. I was in the middle of my email stating, "It seems like every turn I make, someone tells me I should write a book. This just seems too crazy; you know how I read, and I write even worse! Besides, what do I have to share? The only thing I have to offer is talking from one addict to another . . ." And as I was finishing that sentence, it hit me like a ton of bricks: "From one Addict to Another." Holy crap, that's it! That's what He wants. It hit me so hard, I began shaking and quickly sent the email. I couldn't believe how this affected me. All of a sudden, it was plain as day. This is what I have to share, and it's also the title of the book! It was right in front of my face and so obvious. I began to think about what this meant and started to pray and kind of talk to God. I felt everything so strongly at that moment. I asked God, "How am I supposed to do this? I don't know what to do." Then I felt like He was right there at my side, and He responded immediately, "I need you to do this for me." This freaked me out a bit—why can I hear Him inside? I don't get this. Again I said, "God, I don't know what to do or how to do this," and He repeated, "I need you to do this for me. You can lean on me, use me, I will be here to help you." I started thinking of the repercussions of following through with this: My whole story, everything about me, would become public. Everybody would know. I began to think of ways around this: "Well, maybe I can write this under a pen name," and I got an immediate response of "No, you need to own this." This was not what I wanted to hear, but it further convinced me that it was God who was talking to me, because I knew it was absolutely the right answer. Again, I told Him, "I don't know what to do! I can't do this," and He replied again, "I will be here to help you." Then a Scripture passage came to mind: "He who is given much, much will be expected." I began to think of everything that God has done for me and given me, and all that He has forgiven me for. To begin with, there was the fact that I still had my wife and my family after everything I had done. I have met so many men who have done just half of what I've done and they have lost everything. What I have found in the graces that I have received from Him are nothing less than miraculous. I knew deep in my heart that I absolutely had to do this. Yet my head was spinning from what this actually meant and all the ways my life would change because of it. I didn't know where to go from here, but I knew I needed additional help.

First I shared the entire experience with Roxane. She said it all made sense to her and seemed to be precisely what I needed to do. Again I was amazed at how she could be behind something that would likely cause her more pain when my story went public. I remember a priest once telling us that when there is a struggle in our lives or our marriage that if the husband and wife are in agreement on a difficult decision, then it is God's will. For Roxane to be in agreement with something with as much potential impact as this book, I knew deep inside that it was something I had to do.

I was trying to figure out where to go from here. The more seriously I took the idea, the more appropriate it seemed. I am the type of person who, after owning many businesses and being self-employed for the last twenty years, knows how to take an idea or a vision, take control of it, and make it happen. Yet as much as it made sense, this was different. This was completely outside of what I was capable of doing by myself. I said a short prayer to God, telling Him that if this really needs to be done, I need the Holy Spirit to write it for me, to just use me to put it down. This would truly be a book that He is writing through me, because I am not capable of doing this in any way, shape, or form. I was still looking for a way out and thought up a lot of excuses—how busy I was with my business, how I wouldn't even have time to write, and so on.

But I was also starting to trust God and His vision for my life. I was starting to have feelings that my business (which, oddly enough, was an Internet company that sold books—almost a punch line of a joke for somebody who doesn't read) was actually something that needed to go away or drastically change. That was a whole different feeling and thought. But I began to sense that it was something that I needed to end or at least to change the way it operated so I would have more free time. I had already toyed with this thought before, as the business occupied so much of my time that I didn't see how I could get away even to take a true family vacation. Now, this whole book idea inspired me to think about what I was supposed to do with my business and my livelihood. At first, I thought that maybe I should try to make a big surge in effort to grow the business to the point that I could afford to hire higher level staff that I could trust to handle financial decisions and otherwise run the business. Then I could occasionally leave for a week or two and take the time I needed to write.

Undecided what the right move was for the business, I decided to try listing it on eBay at a premium price. I figured if it sold, that was fine; I would have enough money to get by for more than six months, long enough to figure out what I should be doing next. After I had it up on eBay for more than a month, I was still thinking that if it sold, then that's what God wanted to happen. The problem was, I was still emotionally holding on to the business and didn't want to let it go. In retrospect, I realize that my reluctance to let it go had nothing to do with holding on to the actual business but was more about what it represented. It was another part of my life that I had to give up, and in my mind that translated into something else I had failed at and was thus not good enough. So a month after putting it up for sale, I wasn't really willing to let it go.

Instead, I made desperate moves to hang on to it and increase its revenue and value. As I said before, my business sold books online on sites like Amazon and eBay. It was basically an inventory-driven business—the more I had to sell, the more sales I made. I never had a problem getting inventory; the bottleneck was getting the books listed online for sale. It seemed that whenever I had a surge in listing a bunch of books online, I would always have a corresponding surge in sales. Even when I had over 20,000 books listed for sale, adding a mere 300 or 400 books online in a couple of days would produce a spike in sales. So in my efforts to prove that I wasn't a failure in this arena of my life, I decided to push this correlation as never before. My two employees and I were going to try to add 500 to 1,000 books per day to our online inventory for a couple of weeks; my thinking was that this 50 percent jump in inventory would bring a 50 percent increase in sales. I prayed about my plan, asking God that if this is not where He wants me, then make it clear now. Be careful for what you ask for, because He listens and will answer you. We started adding inventory at a very fast pace. In about two weeks, we got the inventory to around 26,000 books. And what amazed me was that rather than sales increasing in a proportionate amount as they always had before, they went down! This blew me away—it was such a shift from the norm that it seemed impossible. Then I remembered asking God to make it clear if this is not where He wants me. Now I said to myself, and in a way to Him as well, "Okay, I get it; I'm done. My heart is out of it." Then without feeling degraded or like a failure, I detached myself emotionally from the business and said, "Let it sell." Within twenty-four hours, my business was sold. I actually had two interested parties at the same time. The experience confirmed that when I get out of the way, God can make what seems like miracles happen in a heartbeat. I accepted this as His will and decided that I would move on, believing that He will guide me where He wants me to go. Today, I am still stunned at how frequently I see God's hand in different parts of my life now that I have surrendered my life to Christ. I also recognize when He is nudging me with His desires for my life.

Yet even with my business sold, I still had reservations and was not convinced that I was really supposed to write the book. I began to meet with various people—spiritual advisors, friends, and so on—to talk about my experience and ask for advice. I was actually looking for someone to tell me that I was crazy and this really wasn't what God wanted me to do, someone who would tell me that this book would cause a lot of heartache for my family, embarrassment for me, and would just be a huge mistake. However, of all the people I spoke to, no one told me this. While everyone seemed to comment on or agree that this would be very difficult, everyone offered encouragement and support for the project.

These meetings went on for several weeks, maybe even a couple of months. While I still didn't know how to begin the book or where to start, I decided to meet with someone who had offered spiritual direction for many people I knew and who I regarded as a person with great insight and a strong relationship with God. I told him the story of how the book idea came to be, as well as what had happened with my business, and I explained that I didn't know where to go next. Without hesitation, he said, "What you need to do is take five days, and on each day spend one hour in adoration and then two hours writing. And at the end of those five days, you will know what you need to do." I was kind of taken aback at how quickly he responded and how sure he was about what to do, even though that's why I wanted to speak with this person in the first place—I had assumed I would get such an answer.

I followed his directions and started the following week. It was amazing how ideas and direction just flowed. In addition to feeling like I was led about what to write, I was also led in many other areas of my life—discovering parts of my history that would help explain some of my behavior.

One of the first topics I was asked to write about was my pain and the pain I have caused others. I knew this was being "inspired" because it surely was something I would not choose to delve into. It's the core of my reality and something I did not want to see myself, much less share publically. Strangely enough, I did start with this and it sparked the beginning of the book, but as God has it planned, I wasn't able to finish the topic until a year later. This initial writing eventually ended up being moved to a section much later in the book. But by the time I finished writing it, I had gained so much more insight into myself and my addiction—something that I hope will be of value to share with others. So it was extremely fitting that I started with the subject of pain but wasn't able to actually finish it until much later.

There are several strange things that happened to me while writing this book. As I discussed earlier, I already believed in what Christians call "spiritual warfare." It's a kind of behind-the-scenes battle between good and evil for our souls and we, living in the world, typically never see that battle. It used to be more or less a concept to me; I never really understood it until I wrote this book. I heard someone once say, "If we truly believe in God, then we must realize that we are not human beings having a spiritual experience but we are spiritual beings having a human experience." That really provides the perspective that this life is a temporary stop and that we are truly part of God's creation as our spiritual nature, our souls, long for Him. I have discovered that when one steps out of his normal "safe" life and does something for God that really angers Satan, things in your life can become a little strange. Some would tell me to prepare to be "attacked" by Satan, and attacks are exactly what happened to me.

I knew that writing this book would put me on a path that would change things forever. People would know things about me that are deeply personal, shameful, and downright embarrassing. Many would not even come close to understanding why I would do this. And if it wasn't for the grace of God, and the event I described earlier about when He asked me to do this for Him, I would never in a million years do it.

In the process of writing I would have doubts, as if I misunderstood Him, or even doubt that I was really asked to write this. I would try to convince myself that maybe it was just an exercise for me, and it's not really supposed to get published. I had also discovered that God can take any bad situation, sin, etc., and use it and turn it into something positive.

One example of this occurred about three months after I started writing when I was rear ended in a car accident. I got a concussion and then had post-concussion syndrome— a twenty-four-hour-a-day headache for about ten weeks along with depression. During this time, I was in a mood that didn't care about anything. I couldn't pray; I didn't even have a desire to. I completely stopped writing. I even considered deleting the computer file containing my manuscript and throwing away my notes, since I didn't "feel" the need to write it anymore. I even seriously doubted what had happened and that I was ever asked to write this book. I didn't care about anything. I seemed to not have any feelings at all. I was just indifferent about life, family, church, friends, etc. I felt nothing.

About four months after the accident, I was feeling a little better and decided to attend the annual men's retreat I had attended once before several years earlier (the one where I received the letter from Jesus). Again, at this retreat, there are several talks and then we break into small groups and discuss the topic. I began to "feel" again during this weekend. Also, I was put into a small group where some of the other men had been struggling with sex and pornography. It was immediately clear to me that my inclusion in this small group was no coincidence. God put me there to share my story and to give some encouragement to these other men. By the end of the retreat, I began to feel again that writing this book was something "I needed to do." While I wasn't yet mentally healed and prepared to begin writing, I was again headed in that direction. About six weeks after the retreat, I had new inspiration, some insights from the retreat, and more passion than ever about finishing the book.

A friend told me that the accident I had was no accident but was an attack from Satan! He said somehow the person who hit me was distracted or something and then the accident happened. I wasn't sure that I believed this, but in hindsight and considering that I had almost deleted the book and destroyed my notes, essentially questioning my faith, I seriously considered whether he may have been right. Also now that I have more passion than before, plus some new insights from the retreat, it seemed that God took a bad situation (or even maybe an attack) and turned it into something better. This was truly something to at least consider.

A few weeks after I started writing again, another event happened. With this one, there was no mistaking it; there was nothing to ponder and wonder about like the accident. I was in the process of editing the book and correcting the mistakes that my dictation voice recognition software makes; I was working on the end of chapter that talks about coming home after the biblical counseling where, in the middle of the night, I thought I felt evil spirits in the room. I was reading the part where I was wondering if it was real or not and, as I read this, I felt a strong presence. It was incredibly intense and dark, not visible dark but like an anger darkness. Suddenly I knew that Satan was in the room. I can't explain how, as it wasn't in words, but he made it clear that what I had felt back then was real. They were his helpers, but he was here now, at my side, and he was pissed about what I was doing. I was overwhelmed with this evil. I thought to myself, "Oh my God, he's here. Oh my God, he's here right now. He's not happy. Oh my God, he's here." I could feel him. There was no question; it was way too intense to be my imagination. The feeling was actually physical, almost like a pressure of someone on my left side, very large and close, almost touching me. I had never felt anything like this in my life; it was way beyond fear. I said again, "Oh my God, he's here. Jesus—what do I do?" Jesus answered me clearly, as clear as when God told me He wanted me to write the book. "Come to me," He said. I knew immediately what He meant. I needed to go to the closest place of adoration. Jesus wanted me to come to Him and be in His presence physically. As I got up to leave, I thought about the book: what if the computer crashes or something? I decided to email the manuscript to myself, so it would be electronically available anywhere. On my first try, I got a file load error in the attachment; I tried again, same thing. Then my email application had an error, and I needed to close it and restart. On the fourth try, I finally got the document attached and emailed to myself. It was such a random, strange event that I recognized it wasn't random at all. I then left and went to the nearest Catholic Church, less than two miles away. All the way there I was saying, "God, why are you doing this to me? Why are you letting me see this? Why is this happening?" I asked over and over; I was kind of in a panic. I was so focused on asking God what was going on that I wasn't thinking about Satan at all.

I got to the church, walked in through the breezeway just before the adoration chapel, and then entered the chapel. As I stepped into the chapel, I stopped about ten feet in, paused, and immediately realized that Satan had left me at that moment. He would not enter the same room as the physical presence of Christ. I had been so focused on getting to the church that I had not realized he was still with me, but when I felt him leave me as I entered the room, it was again like being hit with a two-by-four—it was all very real.

As I went to a kneeler right in front, I noticed that there was only one other person in the chapel; it had to be the person who was assigned to be in the chapel that hour, as adoration chapels in general are never left unattended. Only one person there was very unusual for that chapel. I knelt down, and for some reason I started to pray a Hail Mary. About halfway through, the woman in the chapel walked out of the room but left her purse there. I was alone in the chapel, which has never happened to me before and is not supposed to happen. As I finished the single Hail Mary prayer, I began to cry. I started to ask Mary, "Please hold me; please hold me. Just hold me." I felt like a little boy who wanted to crawl up into his mother's lap. I kept saying this over and over for about ten minutes; then the woman came back into the chapel. I pulled myself together, stopped crying, and sat down in the chair. I didn't want someone to ask me if I was all right or anything. I didn't want anyone to know what just happened. I felt a little embarrassed about this whole thing and thought no one would believe it had really happened.

For the next ten to fifteen minutes, I just sat there in silence, not praying, just "being." After that time, everything was very peaceful. It was similar to the feeling I experienced several months earlier after my surrender prayer, though less intense. I felt the Grace of God surrounding me. I left the church and the entire experience was gone. Satan was gone; all feelings of any type of spiritual presence were gone. Everything was normal except for the feeling of an overwhelming peace that remained. I felt safe and protected.

After a few hours, I began to question what had happened. At the end of the day Roxane got home from work, and I reluctantly told her about it. I almost felt silly; it was such a strange event—but it was just too real to ignore. As I told her about my day, I became very emotional and knew at that moment that it was truly real.

It was now Tuesday, the day of my Romans 6 group. I was considering whether I wanted to tell my story that night in the meeting. I decided to print the few pages from my manuscript that I was editing when the whole thing started. I planned to have it with me in case I felt moved to share the experience. As the pages were printing, Bob called me. He said he was sick and needed to cancel the meeting, but then he asked if I needed to talk about anything. I thought to myself, "Are you kidding me? To call me as the pages were printing and ask me if I needed to talk about anything! Could the Holy Spirit be any clearer that I needed to share this and do it right now?" This was absolutely no coincidence.

I told Bob what had happened. I asked him what he thought

and if he thinks it was real. He said, "Oh, absolutely! God's got ahold of you and is making it very clear that this is something you still have to do." I knew he was right; I just needed someone else I trusted to say it.

The first time I attended mass after this event, I had a hard time taking the Eucharist. I always knew in my intellect from the teachings of the church that the Eucharist is the true body of Christ. But now, after my experience, I really, really understood it—I got it. If Satan wouldn't even enter the room with the Eucharist there, it was really the true presence of Christ. He was *really* there. I suddenly felt unworthy of taking the Eucharist. But then I reconsidered: nobody is worthy and never will be, but He wants us to take Him anyway. It was a struggle. For the first time, I truly felt the humility of accepting Christ in this way.

---

A piece of theological clarity: When I shared this experience with a spiritual director, he told me that when Satan left me, it wasn't because he was afraid of the physical presence of Jesus; it was because he knew that he had lost that battle and so retreated. He reminded me that Satan was in the physical presence of Christ during His forty days in the desert and was tempting Him.

---

# Pain

# Chapter 19

## My Pain and the Pain I Caused Others

It was after my affair ended and after I attended the men's retreat where I first made contact with Jesus when the catastrophe of my two worlds—my two realities—really collided. In my mind it was over, I had stopped it, and it was all in the open. I was okay now, so let's move on. Wrong answer! The damage I caused had just begun. I think it's because I was still in such a state of selfishness, self-preservation, self-fulfillment, and it was all about me, me, me, that I was incapable of understanding the pain and hurt I had caused, nor did I want to understand it.

But pain was really the crux of my story. The pain started with me and my childhood. Back then I felt insignificant, as if no one really cared about me, as if I didn't matter, and I couldn't make a difference. Out of my pain and my disconnect with God, my problems developed as I sought to fill the hole in my soul. I didn't go about this in a healthy way. No, instead I developed a full-fledged sexual addiction and in the process inflicted pain on those I love the most in life, as well as others whom I barely know.

Unfortunately, my feelings of low self-worth from my childhood have affected me in still other ways. I have a deep anger that many times makes everything annoy me or piss me off. I carry so much resentment, disappointment, and contempt for myself that I think I project it onto other people.

For example, when a waitress makes a mistake, I think she is incompetent and stupid. When my wife doesn't listen to what I told her or remember the answer to a question she asked earlier, I get pissed off. I think deep down that I perceive both of those situations as being a disrespectful act toward me. I feel as if the people involved didn't have enough respect for me to get my order right or to listen to me. I am brought back to my childhood, and once again I feel insignificant or as if I don't matter.

With such feelings of insignificance and worthlessness, it seems like everything that happens in the rest of the world is about me. Anything that somebody does wrong in relation to me feels like an act directly against me.

When I was a young adult around twenty-five, I was curious if I was really stupid or not, and so I took a test for the elite brain club called Mensa. The results showed that my IQ was over 140 but not quite high enough to get into the club—"Still not good enough" is what I concluded. This thinking is not rational: I have an IQ of over 140 but I still think I'm stupid, not good enough, and generally incompetent! Wow! Talk about a warped sense of self. It's also worth noting that at that time I had no relationship with God.

Looking back, I see that I had developed extensive control issues. It had to be my way; I had to do it; and I had to be the best and excel. This was true to the extent that during most of my adult life, I was very entrepreneurial and had my own companies because then I could act on my own ideas and do things my way to achieve success. I think this drive was also connected to the idea that just maybe I would finally be good enough if I was successful enough. In the last twenty-five years, I have only worked for one company that wasn't mine. For six years I worked there and was the director of a division where I reported to a "hands-off" boss. The division I ran was located in a completely separate building and miles away from the corporate offices. It was just like running my own company—again!

Throughout most of this time, I was married to Roxane, who also tended to be judgmental or disapproving and who (unintentionally) greatly contributed to my feelings of incompetence. She herself had many deep wounds, like me, and thus we kind of fed off each other's negativity, control, and anger. Except for work, for the most part, I felt useless, worthless, not good enough, and depressed. I would generally prefer to just withdraw from life. My addiction—acting out, fantasizing, and so on—really was a drug. I needed it. I craved it. Every fantasy, every magazine, every video, and eventually every massage parlor and prostitute, was the "fix" that I absolutely had to have to survive life. This became my reality—the alternate life and fantasy I needed so much. I held on to it more tightly than real life. Real life was actually an annoyance; it was just something in the way of my created "alternate real life."

So my sexual acting out and my work were my two escapes from everyday life. My entrepreneurial side had generated several companies, all of which "owned" me. I was a workaholic, but work was another place where "I had control." Achieving goals or being successful was another "drug" or "fix" in the addiction. I had no limits on how hard I would push and try to keep going; even when a company was failing, I wouldn't give up. Though many of them did fail and shatter my glass house of control—thereby proving the "truth" that I was incompetent and insignificant—I only had an even deeper need to do it again and try even harder. With every new business start, however, I was once again ignoring my wife and family. This created further complaints and criticism from my wife (justifiably), but actually facilitated my need to escape more into both addictions.

With my companies, I had no real final goal, no end game. I just knew that more was going to make me better and eventually, if I could be successful enough, I would be worthy. It was like plowing forward with blinders—clueless of the damage I was inflicting and the life I was missing. And I did not even have a quantifiable goal that I could reach to prove to myself that I was worthy and good enough. But what would I really be worthy of if I reached my unnamed goal? I never thought about that, never had the goal in mind; I just knew I had to push to get there. I possessed the drive to succeed, the drive to be fulfilled, the drive to be accepted and loved, even if it was imagined or paid for. My actions were so desperate, so destructive, so painful.

Today, what disturbs me most is the pain that I have caused other people. The closest and most regretful is to my family, especially my wife, Roxane. My sexual addiction behavior has torn her up. Toward her, I have been dismissive, disrespectful, and emotionally abusive; I have just dragged her through the dirt. Add on my work attitude and entrepreneurial workaholic behavior, and it is even worse. She was definitely not number one in my life. I really don't deserve to be married right now; most men in my situation are not.

Through this whole process, I believe that Roxane continued to love me. Although her love was buried by intense pain, it was still there. I know that the divorce discussion with Father Ken was about that—she was trying to get permission to run from the pain. And I say permission because she is very committed to her faith, to the church, and to God's will. Divorce is not something you do because things are not going as planned. Marriage is for better or worse, and yes it was the worst for a long time. Yet, through it all, Roxane was still committed to God's will and the church's teaching, even when she was looking for loopholes to run from the pain with a clear conscience. While she was given one, she was encouraged to wait a little longer and she did.

Today I can also see the full fallout from my behavior. My wife, first and foremost, but also my kids were especially affected by feelings of rejection when I moved out of the house. In my role as a father, I had a very difficult time expressing love to my children, and in most cases I didn't do so. While this was not modeled for me growing up and so I didn't know how to be actively loving to my children, the real tragedy is that I didn't even realize I wasn't giving them what they needed. Plus, my unhappiness with myself has resulted in anger that was directed at anyone near me, including my own kids. How insignificant did I make them feel when I projected my pain on them? I can only imagine. I pray that my actions and my failures will not affect their own choices and behaviors; I hope they do not feel they have to prove that they are "good enough." Unfortunately, I can see that in some ways this has already come to pass.

I also recently began to realize how much further the consequences of my actions have extended. While my family was the most obvious casualties of my actions, I imagine that Tiffany and her family suffered similar damage. Tiffany was the woman I had an affair with, and we had the intent of being together until I broke it off. How hurt and rejected she must have felt. Another big one is Tiffany's husband. He had to have experienced much of the same pain that Roxane did. How he must hate me, even after more than a decade has passed. I pray that he can or has forgiven me, because he doesn't deserve to live in that kind of pain and anger; he deserves to be free. I then think about how his anger and resentment may have affected their children and about how the affair affected their children. "Mommy is leaving Daddy for someone else" they were thinking at one time. It's likely they thought that their mommy was going to leave them too. This had to have caused feelings of deep rejection, fear, and panic. Did this emotional stress affect their schoolwork? Probably. It may even have influenced what material they learned and may continue to affect their future grades in future classes and life. The feelings of rejection they experienced may play out in later behavioral issues and may even eventually affect their parenting skills and their relations with their own spouses and families. The stress, anger, and negative feelings that exist in a household when parents are unfaithful have the potential to produce ripple effects that are staggering.

How about the people who knew what was going on in my own company? If an employee viewed me as a respected boss, did I paint a picture that this kind of behavior with acceptable? Did I ultimately make way for someone else to have the nerve to have an affair? If ten people in the office knew, nine knew I was an idiot. But one may say to themselves, "If he can do it, why can't I?" thus starting another chain of damage like mine.

While it's impossible to know the exact effects of my acting out, what is certain is that what I have done *will* affect generations of people, and I can't stop that. How many people have I screwed up?

# Chapter 20

## Why Did God Allow This?

I look at what I have done and truly wonder how God allowed me to do this and cause the resulting damage and devastation, all through my own selfishness. The pain and desperation I felt were so deep that I completely ignored God and acted solely to soothe my pain, without realizing what I was really doing. I was so focused and needy that I was blind to virtually everything around me. This was true even though I didn't consciously know that the pain existed or that my actions were an attempt to satisfy the pain of emptiness, worthlessness, and craving of true love and connection.

God gives us free will. It's the most precious gift we all share. God can do anything, *except* interfere with our free will. Even so, He will nudge us, put obstacles in our path, and even speak to us if we are quiet enough and can listen; however, this is rare for most of us. In my case, I tended to think that He allowed events to happen because of my pain. And He allowed me to act as I did for forty years, knowing that eventually my back would be against the wall and I would surrender myself in a cry to Him. It was then and only then that I began to hear Him. It was then that He began to act in my life. As I now listen, God tells me that my story and the information in my heart that I share in this book will help others in some way, and He has made it very clear that I need to do this regardless of the shame and embarrassment that I may feel. I also see that my doing this, as raw and potentially embarrassing as it may be, might just be some restitution for the dozens, hundreds, or possibly even thousands of souls that I have damaged or misled. This shame and embarrassment is a tiny price to pay for my wrongdoings.

I believe that what I did and the pain I caused others were not God's will, but since He knew I would do this anyway, He created a plan to turn this evil into good. This was a plan that I would have the free-will choice to accept or decline. And with what He has done in my life, and the forgiveness that I know I have received, I had no choice but to accept his request. I am moving forward with blind trust, as I have no idea where He is taking me. But I know if I let Him lead, that wherever He takes me will be His will, not mine, and can only lead to good things. I pray daily that what I do with this book will help others find a way out of the desperate pit of sexual addiction and discover the ultimate love that they deserve by receiving Christ into their hearts. I have discovered that whenever I surrender my life to Him, things work out so much better and events are positively orchestrated in ways that I couldn't even imagine. Healing and mercy take place in a way that only Christ can touch. It is all clear now why on the day when His desire for me to write this book was revealed, He said to me, "I need you to do this for me." It was powerful, it was scary, but I knew deep in my heart that it was a call and I couldn't say no. I owed it to Him.

# Chapter 21

## I Am Such a Mess—
## How Could God Love Me?

I used to truly believe that God couldn't possibly love someone like me who was such a mess. In my mind, this is why I could never be worthy of God's love: I am too screwed up, too far gone, just not worth it. Perhaps you're familiar with the parable in the Bible where a shepherd loses one of his sheep from his flock, and he spends an endless amount of time and effort to find that one lost sheep, rejoicing when he finally does (see Luke chapter 15, verses 1–7). Even though I was aware of this parable, I nonetheless thought, "That's fine, he will look for the lost sheep in the neighboring town, but I'm so lost that I am in Australia— too far to be worth his time." I actually lived with this belief.

One day I was spending some time with my sixteen-year-old son who, even after everything that has happened, turned out to be very insightful and understanding and is a person of great faith. Somehow this parable of the lost sheep came up, and we talked about how life events affect a person. I shared with him how I felt so lost and feared that I was too much trouble for even God. My son responded:

*Dad, you don't get it! It's like you're playing left field in a baseball game, and your back is to the game and you're looking at the stands full of people. Staring at these people, you can't see the game. You're thinking that you are so far gone, so far out of the game, that you can't even see it. But in fact all you have to do is turn around and the game is right there. Just turn around and Jesus is right there, behind you, waiting for you to turn around and be received into His arms. He's always been there, right behind you waiting for you, but because you had your back to him, you had no clue that you are actually that close.*

These words were so apt, and I knew he was right. This started the pivotal change for me. I knew deep in my heart that this had always been true. Jesus never left me; He's always been there waiting for me to turn around. I know this is absolutely true for every single person who thinks God isn't there for them or who think that they are too much trouble for Him to bother with. Emptying yourself or surrendering yourself is the act of turning around. He is right there, right behind you. He's always there, no matter what, just waiting for you to choose to turn around and be received by Him. There is no action, no sin, no life you can live that would cause Him to reject you if you truly turn around and ask for His mercy to receive you and if you surrender your life to Him. He won't force Himself on us. He just patiently waits for us to turn to Him. And that turn is critical for life.

---

# Addict to Addict

Remember, Jesus sees us with only mercy and grace. The sooner we can begin to see ourselves that way, the sooner we can forgive ourselves and the sooner we can begin to live without self-loathing, without self-condemnation, and without self-judgment. And when these feelings go away, so does a huge portion of the reason we are addicts. When I refused to forgive myself, I was putting myself above God. So my standards were higher than God's? How ridiculous!

---

Another deep struggle of mine was the desire to be loved and wanted. I think this was my biggest need and something that seemed the hardest to meet. I felt so alone, so unwanted and insignificant most of my life. I'm not sure when I developed this false belief, but I thought the ultimate experience of desire was to be wanted sexually by an attractive woman. I always thought God is so perfect, what would He want with me? As a result, I had to be wanted by another person. And for some reason, sex was that experience or expression of being desired or wanted. This of course is a lie, but it's what I believed. It was the goal to achieve at any cost, the false truth that I lived with most of my life.

Then something happened. I heard a couple of things that affected me in a deep way (I think it was one of those nudges from God). In a seminar I was attending, a priest said that God created us for Him. He wants us to love Him. He knows it is impossible for us to ever be perfect or even be worthy of His love, but He chooses to love us anyway. It made sense that Jesus Christ was the only perfect person to ever walk the earth—and He was God's son—and so it is impossible for us to be perfect; it can never happen. But we are His children, His creation, and as imperfect as we may be, He needs us to choose to love Him. That completes the circle. Almost like an electrical circuit, God's part is already there but we must choose to complete the circuit, hence free will.

A few weeks later, the second part that hit me was the line from the movie *October Baby* where the adopted daughter tells her father "Thank you for wanting me." It hit me again. I've been needing to be wanted my whole life and that's what I've been searching for; that's my desire—the desire that I have been in such a misguided way trying to fill. I had just a few days earlier discovered that God created us for Him and that we needed to choose Him—even though we are incapable of being good enough or worthy enough. God chose to create us. God knows before we are born who we are and how we will act. Despite our imperfections, He still wants us. He still wants me. God knows all. God knew before I was born all the sins I would commit, all the people I would hurt, all the pain I would cause others, but He created me *anyway!* And He wants me to turn to Him, to choose to love him. Even though I am one of the most sinful people I know (my perception), He knew this and created and loves me anyway, and He wants me *anyway.* He knows what's deep in my heart and deep in my soul. He knows every sinful thought and action I have committed. Nothing is hidden, I am an open book, and he still intentionally created *me* and wants *me!* All for the purpose of choosing *Him!* I am a deeply selfish and self-centered person, and He wants me anyway! HE WANTS ME! To be unconditionally loved in such a way, that is truly humbling.

# Addict to Addict

When you feel yourself begin to be pulled into temptation, or impure thoughts begin to creep in (and I do mean "begin," because once your thoughts have gone too far, this may not work), try saying this prayer:

> Jesus, I hand you this battle. I no longer keep you away because I feel I am not worthy of you. I accept your full and unconditional love into my heart. I feel the warmth and fullness of your spirit entering my soul. I do not need or desire anything else. I rest in you.

Then just be still and quiet for a few minutes. If you can truly surrender (or empty yourself) and relax, you will not want to leave the place you have gone to. You are in a kind of meditative state and peace should blanket you. This process will take practice.

If you are unable to be still and quiet, maybe because you are at work or somewhere else, you can still achieve a peaceful state. What I do is keep doing whatever business I am conducting and imagine sitting peacefully at the feet of Jesus, just resting there. I imagine this while I'm still shopping or working or whatever, and still just relax in those thoughts. This exercise separates me from the battle and temptations immediately, and if I stay there ten minutes or so, the thoughts and battle leave me for hours, sometimes for the entire day.

This process came to me after it became a naturally

desired process, a kind of "escape." If I had tried saying this prayer when I was living like I wasn't worthy of God's love and I was running from Him, keeping Him away, then this prayer probably wouldn't have worked. But I think if I had thought of this prayer back then or if someone would have given it to me (like I am to you now), then it may have quickened my acceptance of God's love and gotten me to where I am today a little faster.

---

If you live and breathe to read this, then you must know that the same is true for you. God *is* compassion, mercy, and love. We cannot *make* Him not love us, because He already loves us; we can only choose to reject or not love Him. God is incapable of turning His back on us. And yes, when we do the ugly things we do, we break His heart. But He still loves us and will *always* take us back with open arms when we repent and ask His forgiveness! Every time we act out, every time we fantasize, every time an attractive woman gives us the time of day and our minds run wild, it's God and His unconditional, everlasting love that we are truly craving. And only that love will fill the void in our souls, the void the addiction so poorly and desperately tries to fill. Trying to fill the void with anything but God's love is like eating out of the dumpster. This is precisely why every time we act out in our addiction, we only feel regret, disappointment in ourselves, and even further self-loathing. We have gotten sick from eating out of the dumpster. That's what addicts do: continually make the wrong choice. Even when we know better, even when we know what the right choice is, we still make the wrong one! It's a habit; it's faulty neuropathways of the brain; it's addiction!

# Chapter 22

## The Way Out

Through my journey, even though I learned a lot about myself, my addiction, and my relationship with God, I still knew I needed to learn more. Now that I was headed in the right direction, God was clearly calling me to share my experiences with others. I was jumping out of my skin with desire to run to the top of every mountain and yell, "You are not alone! It doesn't have to be this way!" But I needed concrete tools to share my newfound knowledge. My story may be an inspiration (I hope), but I didn't think it was enough.

I had been hearing about an intensive weekend retreat for addicts called "Every Man's Battle." (You can find out more about this program at their website http://newlife.com.) I called them to learn more about the program, and they asked a few questions about me and the short version of my story. Then they told me that since I was not in crisis, it might be more appropriate for me to visit a counselor in the Denver area. By coincidence, this counselor is the one who runs these weekend retreats around the country every month. His name was Jason. So instead of going to the retreat, I started meeting with Jason. And over the next several weeks, I learned a ton of information and tools that helped me define and articulate what I had already discovered—plus a significant amount of additional helpful material. This information also helped me further refine the battle for myself, as well as begin to expose other areas of my life where I was struggling without knowing it. I will share some of what I've learned in those sessions here.

Jason showed me this diagram:

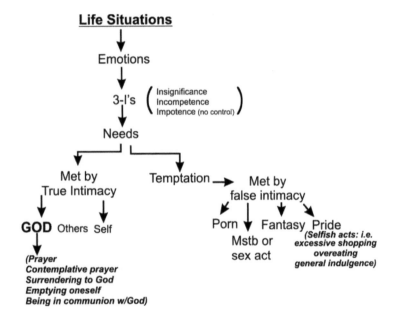

This diagram is very powerful in the battle of sexual addiction and may be useful to people struggling with practically any addiction. The key is the three "I's": Insignificant, Incompetent, and Impotence (which in this case means not being in control). These are three key feelings that we addicts struggle with and that lead us to try to overcome them by making choices, usually the wrong ones.

One of the keys to healing this process is understanding and accepting that you can't do it alone. You cannot control this addiction. This is critical. You have to realize that the more "you" try to manage or control the addiction, the more power it has over you and the more you will fail. Like those Chinese finger traps kids get at carnivals, the more you fight to get out, the tighter the hold is on you. To get out, you need to relax and surrender. It's the same with an addiction: you have to relax, give up, and surrender. In this case, you need to surrender the cravings to Christ. You also need to replace them with appropriate memories and behaviors or even appropriate healthy fantasies.

Here is an exercise that I started doing that relates to this diagram. I try to work through the exercise three times per day—morning, midday, and evening. Just try to fit these in whenever it's convenient for you. Ask yourself if you're feeling any one or more of these feelings of incompetence, insignificance, or impotence. Write them down and then, in a sentence or two, describe what made you feel this way. If you need to write more, go ahead; just try to write at least one or two sentences.

## Examples:

"My boss pointed out something I was doing yesterday that was wrong. I felt incompetent and stupid."

"My wife had a headache from a hard day at work, and I'm not getting the attention I need right now. I feel insignificant."

"When I was cooking breakfast this morning, I broke my egg yolks. It just pissed me off; I feel like I have no control over this and feel incompetent and impotent."

"It's raining again today and I wanted to go fishing. I have no control over when the weather doesn't do what I want; I feel impotent and out of control."

"My bank account was $0.12 negative and they charged me a $35 fee for this. This is so stupid; it really pisses me off. I know it was my fault, but they don't have to punish me like this. I feel like I have no control, and I feel incompetent because this tiny mistake cost me a lot more money. I also feel insignificant, as if they don't even care about me, the customer."

Now look at the diagram and see how easy it is to go down the right-hand side. We need to be in control, we need to feel important, and we need to feel cared for with some type of intimacy. We have become trained to respond to these feelings by taking control and following the temptation side of false intimacy. When situations similar to the examples given above happen in our lives, we need to fill them with something. We need love and attention, and it needs to be our way. We've learned to reach out to things like pornography, masturbation, fantasizing, or some other act that is prideful and about us. We reach for something that makes us "feel" in control, such as eating, shopping, or many other actions driven by this need. But when examining our feelings and doing this exercise three times per day, we can catch one of these three "I" feelings, recognize its cause or source, and *choose* at that time to go down the path of true intimacy. Typically, the most satisfying and powerful is to choose God for that intimacy. Sometimes just praying to God, even if it's only to vent or complain about what's wrong in your life, is all that's needed. Just dump your problems on Him—He can take it. Prayer doesn't always have to be a holy type of praise or recited prayer to God. The best prayer is just having a conversation with God, knowing that He is the one who truly loves you unconditionally and without fail. It's like talking to the perfect father or the father you wish you had. And in this prayer or conversation with God, you can try imagining yourself handing Him this problem or feeling you're experiencing and asking Him to take it away, because you can't handle it by yourself and you don't want it.

Depending on your religious beliefs, it may be helpful to recognize that Jesus Christ, as the son of God, is really God with a human face. Asking for help and talking to God as Christ is sometimes easier, because you can imagine a real person who cares and has the same power as God. This person can look at you and know what is deep in your heart and soul—the pain and frustration that you experience—and love you more deeply than you will ever know.

Even though these feelings have not turned into sex-related thoughts or acts or desires yet, recognizing the feelings now and purposely taking an action on the left side of the diagram will help to defuse the feeling, bring it to your awareness, and prevent it from taking over and then habitually taking the wrong path. Use this time, even a minute or two, to surrender your feelings to God or Jesus. Mentally hand over those feelings and say, "It's not mine; Jesus, please deal with this." Then recall one of those feelings that brings you moral or good pleasure. Think about that experience and how you felt.

I try to remember the experience that I described earlier about surrendering my addiction for the first time and the resulting sensation of a warm liquid flowing over me that I knew was the Holy Spirit. While I don't experience this exact feeling again, I kind of fantasize, if you will, about the memory of that event. It still does bring peace and relief, just not at the emotional level of the actual event.

Doing this three times per day will begin to retrain your brain to go this way naturally instead of going the sexual way. Ideally, this will catch those negative feelings before you're off the deep end where it's difficult, if not impossible, to get back. Be honest with yourself about your feelings. This is not the place to tell yourself that things don't bother you and you're okay. These feelings are powerful, and they are what have been making you feel out of control and drawing you into the abyss of this addiction. If you do this honestly and routinely, you will see that this works very quickly. It diffuses the craving to go down the wrong path by merely acknowledging the feeling before the desires that you typically fall for takes over. This will begin to correct patterns and habits by rewriting the neuropathways. It will take time—a minimum of many weeks and probably months—but it does work.

Another thing that helps me sometimes is remembering that God and Jesus just want to be in communion with me. That just means to "be" with Him. I think of the story of Martha and Mary (Luke 10, verses 38–42) and close my eyes and think about being like Mary, just sitting at the feet of Jesus. No conversation, no questions, just *be*. Another way to look at this is to try to be like a dog and his master. The dog is content just sitting at the feet of its master, just to *be* with its master. What a great place to be—sitting at the feet of the one who created you, the one who loves you unconditionally for all eternity. There is a feeling of safety and protection and love to just be with God.

Closing your eyes and sitting at the feet of Christ is like surrendering. When I talk about giving it up or surrendering, I don't mean to stop battling the addiction, but rather to have someone with the ultimate power to battle it on your behalf—to separate yourself from the battle. Empty yourself of the addiction and give it to Christ to fight the temptation and battle on your behalf. In the three "I's" diagram, it's the impotence option that is important here. You are out of control, and while it may sound like an oxymoron, you can gain the ultimate control simply by giving up control—again, to surrender the feelings, the battle, the desires, and the addiction to Christ. He wants us to do this. This is a very intimate act; surrendering something this deep within us to Him creates an intimacy that will change your life in ways you can't even begin to imagine.

# Chapter 23

## Continuing the Battle

At this point in my recovery, I "see" the battle before me, not just thoughts as part of my life. I know that for me, the more I see and the more God has revealed to me, the more intense the battle attacks have gotten. This further proves to me the existence of spiritual warfare—the battle between God and Satan (the fallen Angel) for our souls. The devil doesn't make us do anything; he can only tempt us or inspire us with thoughts, ideas, or suggestions. We have to choose to take action. Yes, we have a choice. But what's behind that choice is what drives us. Our history, our needs, our weaknesses, and so on are what commonly lead us to the wrong actions. Addicts so desperately need to fill a void or emptiness that it overwhelms us to the point of powerlessness. When I'm tempted with thoughts that come into my head, I "see" the attack is coming from outside. But it's still an attack, still a temptation. And they can be oh so very strong. And I know these attacks are thrown from the outside, because I know different; I know what they are suggesting is wrong. They're still just as powerful as before I could see them. I would begin to think things like "I feel uptight and I need a release. Some pornography, fantasy, and masturbation would really feel good right now; just a short session won't hurt anybody. Then when I'm done, I will feel better, more focused, and better able to concentrate on my work and I will actually be more productive." I know the thoughts are a lie, so how could they be coming from me? But I *want* to believe them; it sure would be pleasurable. So I can talk myself into believing these thoughts or even ones that lead to more serious actions.

If we ask for it and if we are willing to be open to it and leave it, God will give us the gift to see these battles and attacks. But what goes with it is also the awareness that we must have God at a minimum help us to fight this battle or, even better, completely give it to Him to fight. Hence the line in my prayer "It's not my battle anymore." It is at this point that I also see from time to time that I don't want to give up the battle. I want to give in. It's so powerful and promises so much pleasure and will relieve my stress that I'm enticed with insatiable cravings. Then it becomes pure discipline in humility to choose to be powerless and surrender the battle; this is *hard* and you won't always win! But you begin to win more and more battles in the overall war.

Honesty and transparency is another weapon; this is where support groups help. We admit when we fall. Now I see it as losing a single battle but not the war. In the past I was losing the war and miserably so. There was a time when I didn't even know there was a war. Pretty hard to win a war when you're not in fighting the battles. But because I know God loves me no matter what, and I confess my sin immediately and repent, I can move forward without living in a pit of self-worthlessness and spiraling down into a repeat offense or even a binge of acting out. I will give you a recent example. This is actually so recent that it occurred during the final editing stages of this book, but was significant enough that I had to add it in.

I was planning a trip to Las Vegas for business. Vegas is a battle especially because of my history there. But it's manageable as long as I'm not alone, and Roxane and I were scheduled to go together. Then something changed in our plans and she couldn't go. We talked about canceling the trip entirely, understanding the struggle, but I said I would be fine. I shortened my trip to one night in order to limit my risk there. I was to fly out on a Monday morning and return Tuesday. It was now Wednesday of the week before. Soon enough, thoughts started to creep into my mind of "I'm alone, and visiting those vendors at the show won't take that long. I bet I could have some fun if I wanted to." I dismissed these thoughts as "That's not me anymore." Still, images and memories of what I had done years ago began to creep in. Again I dismissed them, but I began recognizing the battle before me and decided to find a Catholic Church in Vegas that offers adoration, hoping to start there when I arrived and gain some strength. Thursday I began just going with the idea of "I wonder how easy it would be to find something right in Vegas because I had only gone an hour outside of the city to brothels before." Now I was telling myself that I wasn't really going to do anything; I was just curious. I began to Google escort services in Vegas. I started browsing them, looking at pictures and prices. I was thinking, "Oh, that's not bad; it's not as much as I thought, but no matter, I'm using my money for gambling. I don't need to be doing this stuff anyway." I would close the site only to find myself an hour later looking again thinking, "Hmm . . . if I was actually going to do this, who would I want to see?" I looked at some ideas and closed the program, again telling myself this is stupid. This is not who I am anymore. Then I'm thinking, "I'm alone, no accountability. This may be my last chance to do something like this; maybe if I win at the tables, I could use that money for this alternate entertainment." I began to see that my thoughts were getting out of hand—very slowly, tiny lie by tiny lie, tiny deception by tiny deception. I started telling myself that if I would do a little extra prayer time and spend time in adoration while I was there, then this wouldn't get to me. "All I have to do is surrender the battle when I am there," I thought.

By Friday, the thoughts and browsing continued: "Oh, what's it going to hurt? It's my last fling." These thoughts were very powerful. I found it hard to work. My mind would be constantly filled with these ideas, thoughts, and plans. I kept looking at the sites. I realized I had to stop and surrender this now, surrender the temptation of the planning process, but I found I couldn't—I didn't want to. I knew I had to, but I honestly didn't want to. I felt like I was surrounded by an impenetrable blanket of temptation. The only way to stop this was to not go at all. Then I'm thinking, "I can't do that; I can't cancel." I told myself (or, more likely, it was being said to me), "I need this for the future of my business and family, and besides Roxane would be pissed. I spent all this money on airfare, hotel, etc. What a waste. I just needed to suck it up and go—and fight harder when I get there." I couldn't sleep Friday night; the temptations of what I could do were burying me. I couldn't seem to pray, and I couldn't seem to analyze the battle and see what my true needs were that the temptations were attempting to fill. It was like a blanket of illicit thoughts and temptations were surrounding me, and I couldn't escape. I finally said to myself, "If I can't battle this here and now, there is no way I'm going to survive there, in that city, alone." Early Saturday morning, I decided with 100 percent certainty to cancel everything. I was trying to figure out the best way to tell Roxane that I had canceled so she wouldn't get all upset, because she doesn't like to know about my battles; it brings up too much old stuff and fears of what might happen again. Even so, I decided I would just have to tell her what was truly going on—that I was getting attacked and the battle was getting impossible to manage. I would just take the fallout from my wife.

But what actually scared me the most was that when I made the final decision to cancel, *all* the thoughts and temptations instantly vanished. It was like someone had snapped their fingers to just clear them away. It was so clear that this was an attack, and when Satan realized he wasn't winning this battle, he vanished and the attack was over. It felt great and freeing to win and for him to leave, but it scared the crap out of me to know how hard he hit me and how far he took me. I had been ready to do it all! Making the decision to not go was the hardest thing I had ever done in my life, even harder than ending the affair years earlier. And when I told Roxane, she said, "Good! I was worried about you, and I don't care about the money." Totally different from the thoughts I had had, those thoughts that were contributing to my needing to go. Were those thoughts also ones that were placed or suggested? I wonder.

## Addict to Addict

Let's be clear here. For any level of success or progress, you *must* see this as a battle—more explicitly, a spiritual battle. The battle for your well-being, the battle for your ability to act as a person of integrity, the battle for your ability to function with clarity and morality in this world, and, most important, the battle for your soul. In my opinion (yes, it's an opinion), understanding this and accepting this fact is 100 percent critical to having any hope of winning progressively more and more battles in this war—the war that will last for the rest of your life. The minute you begin to feel strong on your own, that is when the enemy will strike and you won't be prepared.

In this process, you must understand your enemy—

Satan. Understand his lies, his cunning ways, and his power. Most of all, understand that you cannot fight him alone. He was created by God and is more powerful than you can even imagine. If you think you can fight him alone, you have already lost. Even a small battle that you're sure you can overcome by your own will, you will lose. Don't even try. But you must understand him and recognize him. I once heard a story about battling Satan. It was likened to a soldier understanding his enemy. Marines were required to take a Russian AK-47 and in the dark disassemble it and then put it back together again. This gave them intimate knowledge of their enemy's weapons. Addicts must do the same with Satan: know his weapons; know what he uses within you to prey upon; and know how he gets to you from the inside out, through thoughts and emotions.

---

What I have said thus far I firmly believe is the required place to be emotionally and spiritually. In the following pages, I will discuss my battle plan. This is what I do only. It is not what I say you should do. As I said before, I am not a trained, educated professional on sex addiction. I'm just like you. One addict to another. There is a lot of information out there offered by counselors, professionals, and other experts in the field, and honestly I am not familiar with more than 90 percent of them. However, considering the material I have read and have learned about in counseling in some way relates to what I have developed on my own. I share this with you as a place to start; follow it to the letter, modify it, or throw it out. I would just say that other addicts whom I have shared this with have found it helpful. Many parts of it are extremely religious, and some parts relate to my Catholic beliefs. In the interest of keeping an easy-to-follow flow, I will repeat other content that I have already written rather than have you jump around in the book to follow.

## My Battle Plan

I divide my growth into three areas:
1. Recognizing when I'm in a battle
2. Developing a recognition of early warning signs
3. Developing a pre-warning sign discipline

I'll explain more detail of each one here before I get into the specifics of fighting the battle.

### 1. Recognizing the battle

This is when I'm actually having thoughts about planning to act out in some physical way—fantasizing for a while, ready to go to the computer, visit a massage place, etc. I'm ready to act. Once I'm here, the proverbial train left the station and it is very difficult to turn around; it's possible but difficult.

### 2. Early warning signs

Here's where I try to recognize the beginning thoughts. Examples may be seeing an attractive cashier at the grocery store and when I check out, she seems very pleasant and makes conversation with me, triggering thoughts that she may be interested in me; I would begin thinking about being in her company, not necessarily sexually but just placing my emotional needs with her for filling them. Or I might see an attractive girl in tight clothes walk by and begin thinking about what it would be like to be with her. If the girl walking the opposite direction in the mall makes eye contact and smiles, my mind immediately jumps to "Oh, she must like me; I wonder what she would be like. Maybe she's really nice and would make me feel good, and then all my problems will go away." Other examples are things like watching TV shows like *So You Think You Can Dance* and seeing the dance moves and outfits that the female dancers wear, which are usually very tight and the moves they make are very provocative.

All of this starts my mind thinking, "I wonder what it would be like to be with her . . ." These thoughts can quickly progress to the desire to act out physically. But if I recognize them, they can be stopped here much more easily than waiting until they progress to physical desires. Personally, I have to guard myself by avoiding certain TV shows that involve dancing. It represents a forward, physically aggressive woman, which I find attractive. Add sexy clothing and I'm in trouble. When checking out at the grocery store, I choose a male checker or an older woman to avoid any possibility of thoughts starting. While I can't always avoid these circumstances, I recognize the possibility of thoughts and work to guard my thoughts before they start. If I do encounter a young, attractive checker who smiles and is chatty with me, I try to turn my thoughts around, changing "She smiled and was nice to me" to "That's just her personality; she's not interested in you ya dumbass. Don't even go there—you know it's crap; you know that's not what you really need anyway." Yeah it's a little blunt, but this is not a battle to be "nice" with.

### 3.   Pre-warning battles

This involves the 3 "I's" that I discussed earlier: incompetence, insignificance, and impotence. My goal (and lack of discipline doesn't always make it happen) is to journal on these feelings three times daily, or at least analyze them in my head. This process can be a game changer. Addressing the true deep issues and rerouting them to God exposes the weakness to you, thus making it less powerful of a weapon for Satan to use against you. Plus the core "need" you have is forward in your mind, creating healing and in time diffusing the emptiness that causes it to be the insatiable craving for fulfillment of outside or worldly methods.

Here is my daily plan.

First thing in the morning—before getting dressed, before breakfast, everything—I say my preset prayers:

*Come Holy Spirit and renew my heart.*

*Dear Lord Jesus Christ, I desire the desire to surrender my heart and my entire being to you but I cannot do it; I fear the abandonment of losing control of who I am. I ask that you take what little space I can open to you, use it, and invade my heart, take it captive, and protect it from all evil. I beg for your help in my complete surrender to you.*

As I say this prayer, I picture myself sitting at the feet of Jesus and just being with Him and knowing that He wants me to be with Him. Sometimes I may sit here for five or ten minutes.

*Lord Jesus Christ, I cannot fight this battle anymore; I'm done. I hand you the dragon to slay; I hand you the lizard to slay; I walk away; it's yours; I'm done. I can't do this anymore. It's not may battle anymore.*

As I say this prayer, I close my eyes and visually hand Jesus part of my cross to carry for me. He takes it willingly and is happy that I asked Him to help me. He always carries my piece without effort, then puts His arm around me and we walk away. I imagine the feeling of the weight of the addiction gone from my shoulders.

I encourage you to develop your own prayers that work for you and represent what you think may help you.

These prayers are fairly short, and I attempt to say them slowly and think about what I'm saying as I go through them. Rushing through them is like not saying them at all. I have to remember to take the time for the visualization that goes with them.

Then a little later, after I have had a few minutes with my wife and she has left for work and generally after breakfast, I consider the three "I's." I sit and think about each one. I almost always find more than one, sometimes all three, that are applicable to me at that time. This experience took a while to learn and to recognize the deep emotions and feelings behind it all. I have attended many spiritual retreats and have worked with many counselors, all dealing with feelings of the past, and I still had difficulty recognizing these feelings. By doing this exercise, I grew a lot. I commonly find repeat emotions with the same underlying problems too. But that's fine; what's important is that I recognize that they are there and that they cause an emotion and have power that I need to expose if I have any chance of fighting.

Here's an actual example: my eighty-year-old mother was in a nursing home for a week during rehabilitation for a previous issue. She was feeling better and demanded to go home. She called me and said she needed to leave now. I live two hours away, making it a real pain to go up there because I needed to coordinate with doctors and the home for releases, etc., so she could leave. She didn't understand why she couldn't just walk out. She was combative and difficult and critical—all bringing back feelings of childhood. I felt responsible for her not being happy and was blamed for her not getting out right when she wanted. This made me feel small and unimportant. I wasn't good enough because I wasn't giving her what she wanted right now, and she let me know that. She blamed me for not letting her go.

Insignificance and incompetence were both now at the top of the list. Also because I couldn't manage and control the situation to her satisfaction, this made me feel out of control or impotent. So in this case, all three of the I's are at play. Plus during breakfast my wife was complaining about our daughter not taking care of her dishes and started getting on me for the same; then she left for work in a bad mood. I'm sitting here thinking, "Why do I bother with anybody? Nobody cares about me and everything I do is wrong; nobody loves me." It was a nice pity party. Pile on the insignificance and incompetence from my experience the day before with my mother, and now I could just let it brew for a few hours and then go to the computer and act out. But instead I sat and thought about my three I's and which ones were applicable right now (in this case all three). Think about what's causing them. Think about how I felt as a child. Identify all causes. I remember my mom always being in a bad mood and the neighborhood kids not liking her. I take some time, recognize the influence of the feelings my mother caused, and in this case, this is how I think about it. In my mind I act as if I am speaking to Mary, the mother of Jesus, and say,

*Mary, I know that you are my true spiritual mother in heaven and you love me unconditionally. I see my mother here in my life now as a kind of "steward" that was assigned to raise me here on earth. I understand that like all of us parents, she didn't know what she was doing and was doing a kind of on-the-job training. Her anger and dissatisfactions are not about me, now or then. She is the one who raised me, but you are my real eternal mother. And I know that as the perfect, compassionate mother, you forgive me for all my mistakes and love me anyway.*

Then I pray to Jesus:

*Dear Lord, I ask your forgiveness of my mistakes and my dissatisfaction with my earthly mother. After all, I understand you gave her to me for a reason and I choose to honor and respect that. Right now I feel incompetent and insignificant and ask you to help me remember that I am truly neither of those, but loved unconditionally by you. I choose to love you in return. I ask you to fill the voids caused by these feelings and wipe them clean.*

I sit for a minute or two and visualize myself at a childhood age, maybe five or six, a time when I was feeling particularly hurt and insignificant, sitting with Jesus in His lap, under a tree in a meadow. Alone with no distractions, it is as if I am the only concern He has; sometimes I sit and cry in His arms. I may sometimes even take more time and kind of meditate on these thoughts, just "being" with Christ. And typically when I'm done, I will be at peace and go about my day. If I can, I will do this two more times per day.

There are of course times when thoughts or someone I see or an image somewhere will trigger desires, and I will immediately go right past any preparation or warnings. I get blindsided you might say. This is where I'm most in danger. If I've done my three I's exercises regularly as I should, these events don't hit me as strongly. Or sometimes things that usually would get me started have no effect or have an effect for only a second and then I can pass right by them.

But many times I get busy and don't adhere to exercises as often as I should, so these events become more difficult to battle. I do my best to catch them, identify that it is an attack, and try to dismiss usual thoughts of "I want this; I need this; I deserve this; it's been so long; it's not that big a deal—after all, I'm not perfect; just indulge and get past this." At this dangerous place, it's pure choice. The seemingly impossible choice is to do what's right, because the other choice is being driven down my throat by a Mack truck and you just can't get out of the way fast enough. I attempt the prayer "This is not my battle anymore," but if I'm not willing to actually let it go, it won't work. If I'm not willing to hand the battle to Christ to fight, then I will fail because I cannot fight it myself. Sometimes I will make a plea to mother Mary to ask her son to intervene and eliminate the attack. If it's a physical person I can see that sparked the attack, I will look at her and think that our spiritual mother Mary resides in her soul, so any derogatory thoughts about her are about my spiritual mother. That usually will cause enough disgust and embarrassment to break the images. I don't know if Mary as a spiritual mother residing in another woman is sound from a theological perspective, but I choose to believe it because it works. Other times I will just repeat the "Hail Mary" meditative prayer to myself while going about my business. Once I handle the initial impact and can think, then I will think about the three I's and try to figure out what this image or event is giving me: what was so pleasurable, what was it giving me, what was I "really" needing because the physical experience with the person would only leave me empty and guilty, so what did I really want? But this only works after I break the initial stun of the sudden blindside attack.

It took a lot of time, discipline, and practice to develop these "weapons," and it didn't always work in the beginning. But now it does nearly 100 percent of the time. The real key was getting myself to a place that I truly believed the thoughts, what I want to do with regard to acting out, were not what I *really* wanted or *really* needed. They were just mere suggestions and lies about something that would create an empty fulfillment. The lie would come up short in its promises of fulfillment. For a long time I would tell myself that, but then I would still say, "I don't care; I want this anyway." If I'm not willing to change, if I'm not willing to surrender the battle or fight with prayer and redirection of ideas and so on, there will be no victory.

I could not imagine even beginning to fight these battles without believing in spiritual warfare and the true existence of God and Satan. I know a lot of people don't believe this or see things this way. But for myself and others who have had success in battling this addiction, at least ones I have met, they know exactly what I am talking about.

Additional critical steps:

I've spoken to you about my steps with the Marked Men for Christ program, Romans 6, and addiction-specific counseling. By no means are these types of programs to be skipped or ignored. Having the experience of discovering and working on your emotional wounds is absolutely critical to this process of growth and recovery. There are many programs out there of this type; I have only told you about the ones I have firsthand experience with. The Resources section lists the programs and materials that have helped me along the way. Check it out. It is a good start but by no means the only solution. I encourage you to research other options as well, especially material specific to sexual addiction.

# Chapter 24

## To the Spouses/Girlfriends

You have been deceived, betrayed, cheated on, and you probably feel violated and disregarded. You feel like you've been kicked in the stomach. You bounce from being angry and resentful to feeling humiliated and hurt. You may even want to run, thinking it will erase the source of your pain. You feel like you don't know who this person is anymore. How could you ever trust him again?

All of these feelings and reactions are expected and justified.

While I have not personally experienced the feelings that you have, I have been where your male partner, husband, or boyfriend is now. And I can tell you that God gave me a gift several years ago when He presented a glimpse of what you are experiencing, but just a glimpse. I describe this event in chapter 10.

I feel that the most important thing I can tell you is that while what he did drastically affected and critically wounded you and your relationship, his behavior is not about you. It is not your fault. There is nothing you could have done to prevent this, nor is there anything you did to cause it. It's not because you didn't love him enough, not because you didn't give him enough sex, not because he wanted to hurt you, and not because he doesn't love you. It is about him, his wounds, and, ultimately, his selfishness—a selfishness that is out of control. He is trying to fill a void in his heart that cannot be filled with things of this world. Even your love, as great as it has been, cannot fill the void he carries.

Remember, this is entirely his problem and his responsibility to fix. As an addict, he cannot control it out of shear willpower. And he cannot recover from his problem alone. He needs counseling, support groups, and, most of all, a relationship with God. If you choose to move forward with him, your relationship and trust needs to be re-established and healed. It's important that you understand, too, that while preventative actions such as imposing Internet filters or TV rating blocks can help, they will not solve the problem—just like taking the drink away will not solve the underlying problem for an alcoholic. An addict is craving intimate, unconditional love, a love that no human can supply. All of us desire this, but for some, the emotional wounds or past life events have created such emptiness that the desire consumes us. Most of the time, we don't even know it. Only by him doing the work to discover why he acts out, why the insatiable craving exists, and giving those wounds and cravings to God can he begin to heal and develop a healthy understanding of what sex is all about. When this happens, he will be a better husband or partner and a better man in many ways.

Whatever you do, do not downplay your pain and, most of all, do not bury or ignore it. You have been seriously wounded and that wound needs attention. Whether you continue the relationship or not, it's important that you work through your feelings about his acting out and the damage that it caused; these feelings need to be resolved. You do not deserve to be stuck with the anger and bitterness that you likely have. It will destroy your life, and you don't deserve that—it wasn't even your fault! I also recommend that you seek specialized counseling to work through what he has done to you. Even if you choose to leave the relationship, counseling can provide the healing that is critical for you to live a life without resentment and anger, which will destroy your happiness and ultimately take a toll on you physically. Although only a small number currently exist, women's support groups can also be very helpful, I have been told. Contacts or recommendations to such group can usually be found through your local church.

In time, when you understand it and are ready, the ultimate gift to yourself is forgiveness. Forgiving him does not excuse the behavior; it does not sweep it under the rug; it does not mean you turn your back on what he does from now on; and it does not give him permission to repeat the addictive acts. He still needs to be accountable for what he has done, both to you and to God. No, forgiveness is not about him but about you. When you forgive him, you are in essence releasing him from having that kind of power over you and thus causing your pain. In this way, forgiving frees you.

With the proper help, a lot of work, and serious changes in his life, he can change. Even if he doesn't, you can heal.

# Chapter 25

## To My Wife

Dear Roxane,

I can only imagine the pain that I have caused you over the years. You did absolutely nothing to deserve this. I cannot apologize enough for what I have done, and you know that apologies have been difficult for me. The dual reality of this addiction made it extremely difficult to face my behavior and the consequences of it. Combined with pride, I just couldn't fully admit what I had done and the destruction I caused—even to myself. I had to hide my pain and disgust with myself with anger that only served to hurt you even more. I truly wish I could do it all over again. Thank you for staying with me and enduring the pain. Thank you for praying for me all these years. You have been cheated out of a good husband and the good marriage that you deserve. I pray every day that God will help me to be the husband you deserve.

You're my Angel. God gave you to me, as He knew no one else could endure the pain I would cause. You tell me that you are not perfect so you can't be an angel, but it's clear to me that, to still be here after twenty-five years, you have to be. God has asked me to write this book both for me and I think to help others. I dedicate this book to you. For without your love, I would not be where I am today.

Love,
Dann

# Epilogue

Where am I today . . . am I cured of sexual addiction? The simple answer is no. The complicated answer is "I don't want to be." The simple fact is that, like an alcoholic, I will always be in recovery. With this addiction, Satan will always try to make me fall. He knows right where to hit me and when to do it. I will always have to be on guard of my thoughts, what I look at, and what I do with that information. I will always need to turn to Jesus for help and to more completely surrender the battle to Him. I need to empty myself of the temptation, the addiction, and anything attached to it. This leads me to the more complicated part. When I say "I don't want to be cured," I might sound insane. Well from the outside it seems that way, but in reality, through my addiction I have found profound peace, humility, and grace, as well as power in my relationship with Christ—especially when I turn the battle over to Him. That is something I don't want to give up, ever. Earlier I described my prayer of the "desire to desire to surrender." Well, since I have prayed that daily and it is a prayer to do God's will, He answered in a huge way. When I successfully surrender the battle, as well as other aspects of my life, I feel an immense sense of peace as well as the power of God working through me. My love for Christ has grown so strong that I *need to need Him.* I crave that peace and strength when I surrender to Him. If the battle of the addiction were gone, I fear that I would not need Christ anymore, and the thought of not needing Christ scares me more than the addiction does. I need Him, I want Him, and I want to surrender every piece of my life to Him, and my addiction pushes me to do just that. No, I don't wish to act out on the addiction, and when I do occasionally become selfish and fall, my life has to stop until I can confess my sin, do penance, and reconcile my relationship with Christ. He is "home" for me.

While things with Roxane aren't perfect today, I think we have an even better marriage now than we did in the beginning. We still have a long way to go, but at least I can go forward. I think going through what we have and surviving it has made both of us stronger, and we understand each other better than we would have otherwise. We both have more compassion for the struggles of other couples that we see in trouble. I have a great desire to help them and I hope someday Roxane will too.

# Appendix

Excerpt from *The Great Divorce* by C. S. Lewis, pp. 98–103. Reprinted with permission.

C.S. Lewis wrote:

I saw coming towards us a Ghost who carried something on his shoulder. Like all the Ghosts, he was unsubstantial, but they differed from one another as smokes differ. Some had been whitish; this one was dark and oily. What sat on his shoulder was a little red lizard, and it was twitching its tail like a whip and whispering things in his ear. As we caught sight of him he turned his head to the reptile with a snarl of impatience. "Shut up, I tell you!" he said. It wagged its tail and continued to whisper to him. He ceased snarling, and presently began to smile. Then he turned and started to limp westward, away from the mountains.

"Off so soon?" said a voice.

The speaker was more or less human in shape but larger than a man, and so bright that I could hardly look at him. His presence smote on my eyes and on my body too (for there was heat coming from him as well as light) like the morning sun at the beginning of a tyrannous summer day.

"Yes. I'm off," said the Ghost. "Thanks for all your hospitality. But it's no good, you see. I told this little chap," (here he indicated the lizard), "that he'd have to be quiet if he came—which he insisted on doing. Of course his stuff won't do here: I realise that. But he won't stop. I shall just have to go home."

"Would you like me to make him quiet?" said the flaming Spirit-an angel, as I now understood.

"Of course I would," said the Ghost.

"Then I will kill him," said the Angel, taking a step forward.

"Oh-ah-look out! You're burning me. Keep away," said the Ghost, retreating.

"Don't you want him killed?"

"You didn't say anything about killing him at first. I hardly meant to bother you with anything so drastic as that."

"It's the only way," said the Angel, whose burning hands were now very close to the lizard. "Shall I kill it?"

"Well, that's a further question. I'm quite open to consider it, but it's a new point, isn't it? I mean, for the moment I was only thinking about silencing it because up here—well, it's so damned embarrassing."

"May I kill it?"

"Well, there's time to discuss that later."

"There is no time. May I kill it?"

"Please, I never meant to be such a nuisance. Please— really—don't bother. Look! It's gone to sleep of its own accord. I'm sure it'll be all right now. Thanks ever so much."

"May I kill it?"

"Honestly, I don't think there's the slightest necessity for that. I'm sure I shall be able to keep it in order now. I think the gradual process would be far better than killing it."

"The gradual process is of no use at all."

"Don't you think so? Well, I'll think over what you've said very carefully. I honestly will. In fact I'd let you kill it now, but as a matter of fact I'm not feeling frightfully well to-day. It would be silly to do it now. I'd need to be in good health for the operation. Some other day, perhaps."

"There is no other day. All days are present now."

"Get back! You're burning me. How can I tell you to kill it? You'd kill me if you did."

"It is not so."

"Why, you're hurting me now."

"I never said it wouldn't hurt you. I said it wouldn't kill you."

"Oh, I know. You think I'm a coward. But it isn't that. Really it isn't. I say! Let me run back by tonight's bus and get an opinion from my own doctor. I'll come again the first moment I can."

"This moment contains all moments."

"Why are you torturing me? You are jeering at me. How can I let you tear me to pieces? If you wanted to help me, why didn't you kill the damned thing without asking me—before I knew? It would be all over by now if you had."

"I cannot kill it against your will. It is impossible. Have I your permission?"

The Angel's hands were almost closed on the Lizard, but not quite. Then the Lizard began chattering to the Ghost so loud that even I could hear what it was saying.

"Be careful," it said. "He can do what he says. He can kill me. One fatal word from you and he will! Then you'll be without me for ever and ever. It's not natural. How could you live? You'd be only a sort of ghost, not a real man as you are now. He doesn't understand. He's only a cold, bloodless abstract thing. It may be natural for him, but it isn't for us. Yes, yes. I know there are no real pleasures now, only dreams. But aren't they better than nothing? And I'll be so good. I admit I've sometimes gone too far in the past, but I promise I won't do it again. I'll give you nothing but really nice dreams—all sweet and fresh and almost innocent. You might say, quite innocent. . . ."

"Have I your permission?" said the Angel to the Ghost.

"I know it will kill me."

"It won't. But supposing it did?"

"You're right. It would be better to be dead than to live with this creature."

"Then I may?"

"Damn and blast you! Go on, can't you? Get it over. Do what you like," bellowed the Ghost: but ended, whimpering, "God help me. God help me."

Next moment the Ghost gave a scream of agony such as I never heard on Earth. The Burning One closed his crimson grip on the reptile: twisted it, while it bit and writhed, and then flung it, broken backed, on the turf.

"Ow! That's done for me," gasped the Ghost, reeling backwards.

For a moment I could make out nothing distinctly. Then I saw, between me and the nearest bush, unmistakably solid but growing every moment solider, the upper arm and the shoulder of a man. Then, brighter still and stronger, the legs and hands. The neck and golden head materialized while I watched, and if my attention had not wavered I should have seen the actual completing of a man—an immense man, naked, not much smaller than the Angel. What distracted me was the fact that at the same moment something seemed to be happening to the Lizard. At first I thought the operation had failed. So far from dying, the creature was still struggling and even growing bigger as it struggled. And as it grew it changed. Its hinder parts grew rounder. The tail, still flickering, became a tail of hair that flickered between huge and glossy buttocks. Suddenly I started back, rubbing my eyes. What stood before me was the greatest stallion I have ever seen, silvery white but with mane and tail of gold. It was smooth and shining, rippled with swells of flesh and muscle, whinneying and stamping with its hoofs. At each stamp the land shook and the trees dindled.

The new-made man turned and clapped the new horse's neck. It nosed his bright body. Horse and master breathed each into the other's nostrils. The man turned from it, flung himself at the feet of the Burning One, and embraced them. When he rose I thought his face shone with tears, but it may have been only the liquid love and brightness (one cannot distinguish them in that country) which flowed from him. I had not long to think about it. In joyous haste the young man leaped upon the horse's back. Turning in his seat he waved a farewell, then nudged the stallion with his heels. They were off before I well knew what was happening. There was riding if you like! I came out as quickly as I could from among the bushes to follow them with my eyes; but already they were only like a shooting star far off on the green plain, and soon among the foothills of the mountains. Then, still like a star, I saw them winding up, scaling what seemed impossible steeps, and quicker every moment, till near the dim brow of the landscape, so high that I must strain my neck to see them, they vanished, bright themselves, into the rose-brightness of that everlasting morning.

# Resources

These are organizations and books that I have personal experience with. A much larger list of current resources is on my website at addict2addict.org

## Organizations
**Marked Men For Christ** (markedmenforchrist.org)
Note: Marked Men for Christ is not a porn or addict specific group but an organization that offers a life changing experience and follow up that will help any man transform his inner pain.

**New Life Ministries/Every Mans Battle** (Newlife.com)
This organization offers books and it most powerful offering for us men is a weekend especially for sex addicts that will change your life.

## Books/CD's
*Facing the Shadow* by Patrick Carnes, Ph. D.
*Winning the Battle for Sexual Purity* (Audio CD set by Christopher West)

## Blog
A blog for comments and communications for recovering addicts will be available at addict2addict.org